Master the Nano
A step-by-step guide to making a no-budget feature film

Shawn Whitney

Copyright © 2019 Shawn Whitney

All rights reserved.

ISBN: 9781694873088

You can do this! Don't let anyone tell you otherwise.

CONTENTS

	Note on terms	i
1	Film Midwife to Film Mama	1
2	Going to Market & Other Lies	6
3	Make Free Valuable	9
4	Enthusiasm Rodeo	13
5	Prior Planning Prevents Permanent Panic	26
6	These Boots Were Made For Walking	38
7	It Ain't Over Yet, Baby	47
8	Spread The Love	51
9	Bring It Home, Send It Away	57
10	The DIY Film Career	67

A NOTE ABOUT TERMS

In the book I often use no-budget, microbudget and nano-budget interchangeably. I realize that this is a bit inaccurate. Typically a microbudget is classified as a film made for less than $250,000 or, sometimes, less than $150,000. I think that nano and no budgets are used interchangeably but it's possible that some accountant somewhere has given them specific cash values. For my purposes I'm using all three to mean teeny tiny budgets that are raised by the filmmakers themselves with little in the way of formal, outside investment, if at all (other than, say, donations of food or gear). The exact cost of your film will be determined by your financial situation and your movie. Labels aren't that important.

1 FILM MIDWIFE TO FILM MAMA

My wife, myself and my producing partners have now shot two films. The first went on to win three awards and go to 8 festivals internationally. The second is in the final stages of post-production and we're in development on our third film, which we hope to shoot in 2017. Not bad considering that we are doing it outside of all the usual channels and reliant on no one's initiative or permission but our own.

Giving birth really is a good metaphor for making a film. There is a lengthy gestation period, involving impatience and discomfort as the project develops. Then there is an incredibly intense birthing process through the production, followed by a lengthy period of "education"; shaping your film to be the best it can possibly through editing, music, color, etc.

For several years my role in this process was one of midwife – or rather, a small part of a team of midwives. I have worked for the past 8 years professionally as an "executive story consultant". Amongst other things that has involved story editing other people's scripts to help them be the best that they can be before going to camera. I say small part because, it might surprise you to know, the creative quality of a script is only one – and not nearly the most important – in getting a film project off the ground.

SAME OLD, SAME OLD

Film, even indies, are an expensive operation, costing in the range of millions to tens of millions of dollars. Investors, whether individual or institutional, want to make their money back and make a profit. And most important to that goal are market elements – "bankable cast" who have face and name recognition in as many countries as possible; concepts that are "fresh" but recognizable (the joke phrase for this being "make it the same, but different"), etc. That's why you see the same actors in movies that follow the same basic plot lines and have the same story elements so often. It's also why retreads, remakes and sequels are so popular. They have brand recognition, which makes them easier to market.

It's also why it's so hard to break in. Investors don't like to take chances with their money. They aren't interested in new voices and new faces or new directors. And fear of risk also makes them prone to irrational prejudices, not just "rational market calculations" as they would have you believe. That's a risk that's hard to overcome if you don't have personal connections. And its one of the reasons why the traditional path is for people to work their way up through either lower level jobs or through other less creative parts of the industry, like making commercials or industrials – to prove their mettle and skill. But that process, as I've found out from personal experience, can take years and years, even decades. And you may well spend all that time and *still* not be seen as a credible risk to helm a feature film.

GLASS CEILINGS

If you call up a sales agent and try to get pre-sales to finance your film (the act of selling your film before it's made to distributors in multiple territories in order to finance that film) one of the first questions that a sales agent will ask you is: "Who is your white, male lead?" Not that all sales agents are racists or sexists but there is a self-perpetuated myth in the film industry that the only actors who will "sell" in international markets are white guys of a certain age. Which is also used to justify lower salaries for non-white guys. (This is a myth by the way if you look at actual film numbers but it is a powerful one). Like I said, high stakes profit motivation leads to irrational prejudices, not as a personal failing per se but as a product of the whole model.

The next question might be about who your director is – are they a man or a woman? Only 7% of the top 250 films in Hollywood are helmed by women, despite all the talk in recent years about overcoming this gap. This is partly because of unconscious biases, partly because producers tend to hire the same people they've hired in the past – and partly because of a belief amongst some that women are less reliable and have more needs that cost money (like childcare).

I'm a white guy but I came into the industry with no personal or family connections, no access to investment funds or banker uncles. White guys do best but not *all* white guys. It's still extremely hard to break in for anyone not already in.

And, so, after years and years of playing the role of midwife, I finally decided to stop waiting, forget about Hollywood, and just start making movies. And what I discovered was that it was possible without selling your house or incurring a 30-year debt. And I discovered that we weren't the first – others had done it and made great films: the Nouvelle Vague Movement, Dogme, mumblecore and more. That means that you can do it too!

2 GOING TO MARKET & OTHER LIES

If you read many screenwriting books or talk to producers or go to film school you will often hear that you should know what sells in the market and write for the market. The American Film Market puts out a fact sheet on which types of films are selling best in any given year to point people in that direction. Film is an industry and industries make products to sell at a profit. If your film doesn't have the potential to make X millions of dollars, using past trends and "market intelligence" few producers will be interested in making your film, few financiers in investing in it.

FUHGEDDABOUTIT

I have taught screenwriting at university and have many screenwriter friends and colleagues. Almost everyone tries to write films that will sell: action movies, romantic comedies, horror, thriller. I've done this – I wrote six "woman in peril" thrillers for a broadcast output deal that was "guaranteed" and which never panned out. Now I have five (one got made) crappy, boilerplate scripts that took up the better part of a year of my life and led nowhere.

And that's the thing: there's 100,000 spec screenplays registered every year with the Writers Guild of America, waiting to get read (which probably means tens of thousands of others that don't get registered). Most of them are "saleable" genre scripts, written for the market. They almost never get read, let alone produced. This year there will be less than 100 spec screenplays purchased in Hollywood. Those are pretty long odds. I once, before everyone used email to correspond, sent 250 query letters to agents in LA, asking if I could send them my script. I licked a lot of stamps. One agent replied and I sent my script. I never heard from her again.

So forget about writing for the market in the hopes that your script will be the one that somehow gets read. At the very least, don't make that your only film career plan.

NO CONTEST

I feel the same way about submitting for contests. You can spend hundreds, even thousands, of dollars in entry fees. Most contests don't even give you feedback or they charge you extra for feedback. Or the feedback is written by interns who have less experience than you and are putting their own frustration at not being able to get their films made into their critique of your script. One contest I entered didn't even send out a notice about who had won and I had to write them to find out.

You could easily spend $5000 on contests over a period of five or ten years if you submit to between 5-10 contests per year. For a little bit more money you could turn your screenplay into an actual feature film. Which is more effective? Which is more rewarding?

OK, enough of being a big downer.

FREEBIRD

One of the freeing things about writing a microbudget film is that the stakes are lower. If your film doesn't sell in China or Germany and make millions, nobody is going to lose their shirt. Instead of trying to write a script for a film that will star Matt Damon and make $50 million (unless you know Matt Damon, in which case, introduce me) you can write a story that you're passionate about and only needs to make a few thousand dollars to break even.

It's about you as an artist and your artistic vision. It's about the stories that matter to you.

Imagine the worst-case scenario: you write a weak script and make a weak movie. It doesn't get into any festivals and the only screenings are ones that you organize with your friends and family, and the friends and family of the cast and crew. In total, 200 people see your movie.

Compare that to sending out queries for years that get no replies. Or entering contests and spending thousands just to get surly feedback that leaves you depressed and drinking too much scotch.

You will have a movie. You will know how to make a feature film. You will have learned important lessons for your next film – how to use dialogue more effectively; how to not "cross the line" while shooting; how to create emotional beats in your story. You will have built relationships with crew and cast. You will have spent a tiny amount compared to going to film school and you will have a feature film credit that you can put on imdb.com (the website where movie credits are listed and popularity ranked).

Mark Duplass shot his first film for $65,000 and it was, as he described it, "dog diarrhea". He and his brother didn't give up. They went on to make movies for about a fifth of that amount that got play at prestigious festivals, including SXSW. They now make million dollar movies and have a TV series, *Togetherness*, on HBO. When Jean Luc Godard made Breathless for under $100K everybody was talking about how terrible it was before it was even released. He was breaking all the rules of film form that were market proven. That film changed cinema history.

Write for yourself, write your passion. Forget the market.

3 MAKE FREE VALUABLE

When you make a movie, even a microbudget, everything costs money – whether it's salaries, gear, materials or food for cast and crew. There's only one thing that's free – writing the script. But just because it's free and just because you're not writing for market doesn't mean you shouldn't apply the same amount of discipline to this part of the process. It's a truism that you can ruin a good script by shooting a bad movie but it's almost impossible to make a good movie from a bad script. Don't prove the truism correct.

The greatest number of person-hours you should spend on making a movie should go into script development. Writing is rewriting. And once you've rewritten it as much as you can, get people to read it, lots of people – people who know scripts, people who don't. Don't get them to all read the same draft: get some to read your second draft – then make changes. Then get others to read your third draft and so on.

BETWEEN THE LINES

That doesn't mean that you take everything that they say and put it in the script (or take it out). You have to learn how to listen not just to the specifics of what they say but also to the general points. Sometimes a reader will tell you that they'd like to see more of the background characters but the problem they're pointing to is not that the background characters need more of a role – which could confuse and dilute your story – but that your lead character is less interesting than your background characters; maybe they're passive and don't drive the plot; maybe they have motivations that aren't as strong as those of your minor characters. In other words, think critically about the feedback.

And once you've gotten as far as you think you can go with feedback and rewrites, organize a reading of your script with actors (or non-actors if you can't get any actors). Listen to how it sounds, particularly dialogue and pacing. Do characters drone on and on? Does it feel boring and flat right in the middle? Mostly just listen and don't take a lot of notes during the reading. You want to hear it. And afterwards get feedback from the readers. Don't respond and try to defend your choices. Just listen and say thank you – unless you need clarification of a comment from one of the readers. You're not trying to defend your script, you're trying to learn how people react to it. Expect them to tear your script to shreds. You've invited them to critique your script and that's what they'll almost certainly focus on – not on patting you on the back. Don't take it personally. If possible have refreshments and socialize at least a little after the reading. Often you can get more useful information in casual conversation than in the formal discussion.

THE GREAT ACT DEBATE

Three-act structure gets a bad rep. Blame Hollywood. They have perfected the three-act machine to drain the life and edges out of scripts – catalyst happens at 12 minutes, first act change at 22 minutes, B story introduced at 30 minutes, etc. But this is in part because the three-act structure is such a powerful and simple machine for storytelling. That is, simple to say or analyze – not so simple to do well.

When I teach screenwriting I'm a very strong advocate for students learning to tell stories in three acts. Even if you want to stray from that structure – and an advanced writer will often learn how to create story structures that fit the types of story and themes that they're exploring – there are key things that you achieve by telling a story in three acts.

Three act stories are premised on the lead character, whether it is a dog, a city or a person, changing through their experience. It is premised on that change being motivated by conflict. And it is premised on the fact that the success or failure of that transformation is rooted in the ability of the lead character fulfilling your underlying theme – love conquers all; in war there are only victims; the wages of sin is death; et al. Without a theme your story has no soul. Stories without soul are like watching a plumber fix the kitchen sink. There's lots of obstacles. There might be rising action and even tension. But in the end it is boring and particular (ie. it's only exciting if it's your toilet that exploded). Good stories have themes that are universal. And a theme, at its most basic, is an argument about what constitutes the good life, as Aristotle put it about politics, whether that be in the positive or negative sense. In *American Beauty* the pursuit of the American Dream is shown to not provide the good life. In *The Secret Life Of Pets*, it is friendship that makes life good and solves problems. A story is a polemic though often we don't notice that its making an argument because it's relying on common assumptions and prejudices. It can seem merely natural. Of course love conquers all, everyone knows that. That's why Meg Ryan and Tom Hanks hook up in *You've Got Mail* even though they are enemies. And it's why Bradley Cooper and Jennifer Lawrence not only hook up but resolve their mental health problems in *Silver Linings Playbook*. Love overcomes capitalist competition AND bi-polar disorder!

Finally, telling a story in three acts at its most basic means being locked into the idea that your story has a beginning, a middle, and an end. It helps keep it from wandering aimlessly. And every good story has a beginning, middle and an end. That is true whether it has two acts or five acts; whether it moves forward through time, backwards through time or jumps around in time. A story is a journey.

ENOUGH ABOUT STORY, LET'S TALK STORY

OK, I'm bogging you down with story theory. But what you really want to know is what kind of stories work best for microbudget films. With advances in technology and depending on your access to the skills, you can really do almost anything now. The 2016 film *Dinner With The Alchemist* is a period film set in early 1900s New Orleans and they shot it for $40K using green screen, archival photos and a strategically placed horse. But I want to suggest that for your first film you should keep it pretty simple and not break your teeth trying to make a Star Wars fan film for $10,000. Here's a few key principles to keep in mind:

Few locations. There's a reason why so many low budget horror films take place in a house and it's not just because ghosts like to haunt them. All you need is one location, five disposable teens, and a monster/serial killer/walking shark. If you're going to shoot 75-90 pages in 10-15 days you don't want to have to have four unit moves per day, where you drag all your cast, crew and gear from place to place, have to set it up, re-light, change costumes, etc. You can cheat this a bit by merging locations. In our first film we used a room in the main house where we were shooting (my house) and dressed it like a lawyer's office. Then we knocked off a couple of establishing shots outside a real lawyer's office of the hero entering and leaving. Nobody noticed.

Few characters. Less people to pay, less people to feed, less people to make up and costume and keep track of. Often times that means in the rewriting process finding characters who play similar dramatic functions and merging them together into a composite character. This can be a good exercise in any case as merging similar characters can give you stronger characters overall. I recently read a script where a supporting character played a mentor role to the hero. Then she disappeared and another character started playing the exact same role. Those characters should be just one.

Few pages. Do yourself a favor and keep it short. Don't write a 120-

page script (in my experience 9/10 long scripts are weak anyway because they haven't done the work to find the core of their story). Mumblecore films were generally under 90 minutes and *Kissing On The Mouth* was 78 minutes. Generally it's about 1 minute of screen time for every page. Try to keep your script under 90 pages. If you shoot 6 pages per day and shoot for 15 days, that's 90 pages. We had a few 12 page days on *A Brand New You* and they were brutal, forcing us to shoot some scenes from one angle in three takes. There were enough scenes that worked that way to do this but you don't want to do that too much. Better to have more time to get what you need.

No stunts/special effects. You can fake a punch here and there. You can even throw in some gunplay and find free muzzle flash effects, bullet strikes, etc. that don't look too cheesy. But you don't want to put in car chases and explosions and space ships, etc. that is going to complicate your life. That half-day with green screen could easily end up eating up your days as you struggle to get it right so that it doesn't look embarrassing. On the other hand, if you have access to a DP who is a pro at green screen or underwater shots, you can consider incorporating it in as an element to bring production value. But you should assume it will take twice as long as your DP says it will to get that underwater love shot that's interrupted by a giant squid.

Centering a story inside one location is a great way to keep it simple and cheap but unless it's key to the story, take it outside a few times over the course of the script. Exterior shots can help your film breathe a bit and not feel claustrophobic or like a cheap sitcom. Shoot a scene walking down a street or in a park.

Avoid uncontrollable elements in your script – like rain or snow. If you get a rain day that will add great texture to your story, take advantage of it. But don't count on it, unless you have equipment to make rain sitting around in your garage.

CONCLUSION

There's lots more to say about writing screenplays and storytelling but this gives you a starting point. Consider reading one or two good books on screenwriting so that you can learn to develop a framework. Syd Field's *Screenplay* is good. I'm a big fan of *Save The Cat* by Blake Snyder, though he is very conventional in his idea of what stories to tell.

4 ENTHUSIASM RODEO

Now you've got an amazing, bulletproof script that tells your passion story without plot holes and missing emotional beats. You're ready for Pre-production! The first thing you need to think about when you've reached this stage is the team. Because the success of failure of any shoot comes down to this. You're going to be asking everyone or almost everyone to work for free. And that means sustaining enthusiasm. To sustain enthusiasm you must be organized and calm. There are, I would say, three parts to your team:

Your production team
Your crew
Your cast
First Things First

Before we go any further there's something that has to be said about working with crew on a microbudget. Chances are you won't be paying them anything, other than the opportunity to gain experience and get a credit.

Be kind to your crew. It's very hard to keep a stable crew for an entire shoot. You're going to lose people and have to fill holes at the last minute when people drop out for paying gigs, other commitments or even just get cold feet. Every film has weak departments. On our last film we kept losing people from production design. It was a nightmare. Our awesome production designer had a full-time art department gig and couldn't be on set most nights. He would leave everything ready and labeled but sometimes wardrobe had to step in to help out. Or a PA with zero experience. Increase your chances of keeping people by giving them the most awesome experience you possibly can.

Don't ever yell at them, no matter how stressed you get. If you need to yell, call an unscheduled break, take a taxi to the nearest field and have them wait while you scream into the night. Seriously. Never. Ever. Lose. Your. Cool.

Take time during set-ups, down times, after getting a shot, whenever you can to tell people individually and collectively what a great job they're doing.

Feed them awesome food every single day. When people get hungry they get grumpy and the fights start.

Throw a great wrap party at the end with free booze and food.

PRODUCTION TEAM

The last thing you want to have happen when you're on set is for you to be the writer, director, producer and production manager. This is a recipe for you to lose your mind. Imagine that your director of photography is struggling to light a scene, the wardrobe department is asking you whether the actor should be in the green suit or the blue suit for this scene and a cop wants to see your location permit.

The key to the success of any shoot is the team. And the producing team should be your first priority.

We were lucky in that we had good friends who were talented but frustrated actors, tired of waiting for callbacks and only making commercials. They were hungry to make a real movie and play real characters and we knew they were reliable because we had a history with them. These kinds of relationships are the first place to start – people who you know and trust who want to be involved in a feature film, whether they are cast and crew.

If you don't know actors or crew or people who want to be producers then you can still find people.

Are there local film clubs, like Raindance, where you can socialize and meet people?

Is there a local film school where you can put up signs? Recent film grads are a staple of indie film production. They're young and enthusiastic and they usually don't yet have the kinds of responsibilities and commitments, like kids and mortgages, that can take them away from your production at inopportune moments. It's even worth contacting film school teachers and asking them if they could recommend students or announce your project in their classes.

Is there a locally focused Facebook film page, like in Toronto where there is a page called "I need a producer/fixer/crew..." which you can request to join and then post for people.

You can advertise for key cast and crew on Craigslist and make it clear that part of this opportunity is that they must be willing to be involved with the producing team. You can also advertise for producers and production managers this way. We found an awesome young production manager/1st AD for our most recent film, *Fucking My Way Back Home*, this way. She also ended up helping us fill in some missing crew, find gear, etc.

One of the things about working with unpaid crew is that there is a lot of turnover – it's a real rodeo trying to keep it all together. That's why it's good to have some people who feel a stake – like lead cast and department heads – beyond just producing. They want the credit and opportunity so they're more likely to stick around.

But it's also good to have someone with specific experience – like a production manager – who will play a dedicated producerly role on set: making sure people sign the necessary deal memos, release forms, call sheets, get your permits, etc. Not that a newbie can't do it but they'll have a steep learning curve, won't have a producer's kit with forms, etc. If you end up having to go with a newbie, I'd suggest dividing up their role between a couple of people and making sure that they have a checklist and keeping on top of them at the start and finish of every day.

In general, you want to have clear roles for everyone on the producing team and clearly assigned tasks from your pre-production checklist. If people aren't assigned tasks, which are then reported back on during production meetings, one person will end up doing everything. That person will be you. It's fine and reasonable for the initiator of the project, and thus its leader, to carry more tasks than others. But don't turn production team meetings into a performance of one.

TO INCORPORATE OR NOT TO INCORPORATE

I hate that art is a product but the reality is that it is. And that means that you need to understand everyone's relationship to that product. That's why you have deal memos and release forms, etc. Those ensure that everyone is clear and prevent (hopefully) future conflict over who has rights to what. But two people have to sign those contracts, one is the crew member, musician, cast person and the other is the producer. But who/what is the producer?

You have basically three choices when it comes to establishing who/what you are? You can go total guerilla, ignore all paperwork and just make your movie. That may be less hassle in the front end but the problem comes if/when you want to sell it. You certainly won't be able to get any kind of distribution deal or get it on any of the typical platforms that people think about: Netflix, iTunes, Amazon, etc. They don't want to be involved in a messy legal fight. They will want to make sure your chain of title documents – indicating that you own the film and that nobody else has any claim to it – are all in order. Festivals never asked us about this sort of thing. And if you just want to screen it for friends or put it up on DIY platforms like Gumroad then this might not be a concern. However, while the demands are less rigorous for chain of title there's still the chance for misunderstanding, especially if the film makes any money. Nothing turns friends into enemies more than disputes about cash.

The next, simplest, model is to set up a single proprietor or partnership business. These are usually simple and cheap and often can be done online in a few minutes. You'll probably also want to do a name search for your company to make sure that great name you dream of ("Miramax is a great name for a production company, guys!") hasn't been taken. This will allow you to assign the chain of title to an entity and grant signing authority to people on behalf of the company. This is still not good enough for traditional distribution, which want to deal with corporations, but it will allow you to hire professional actors. The trouble with this kind of company is that any liability, law suits, etc. are your personal responsibility.

The third, and most challenging option, is to set up a corporation. This is relatively simple in some districts (The Clintons and Donald Trump have about 10,000 corporations located in one building in D.C. because it's easy to do there). But you should get a lawyer to help you with this so that you do it right. A corporation is a person, legally speaking, so if there's liability issues and a lawsuit, it won't be you personally who gets sued and you won't lose your house. It also means a separate tax filing, with the help of an accountant, which is a lot more expensive than filing personal income tax or even business income tax. On the plus side you are more likely to be eligible for traditional distribution (assuming you have all your paperwork in order). What production companies typically do is that they set up a corporation for every single film production, separate from the parent company. This means that liability from one film doesn't bleed into other films or into the parent company itself, shielding them from being ruined by one disastrous film. But that's a bit pricey for a nano-budget film production.

We set up a corporation, primarily because we were told that we had to do so to access the ACTRA (Canada's version of SAG) ultra low budget program (called "TIP"). We wanted to hire professional actors – and two of our producers were the stars and were members of ACTRA so it needed to be an ACTRA set. We were lucky in that one of us had a lawyer for a close relative and he did our legal work pro bono. It was still hundreds of dollars to set up and our taxes cost us hundreds of dollars every year, just to maintain the corporation in good standing, even if we're not making a movie that year. So, this is a decision that you will have to weigh out. I would strongly advocate for establishing, at the very least, a registered company. If necessary, later, you could transfer the chain of title over to a corporation that you establish. That will require more lawyer work and thus more fees but you wouldn't have to pay them unless they become necessary. Talk to an entertainment lawyer.

While we're on the boring but necessary legal aspects – and please note that I'm not a lawyer so you should take everything I say with that in mind – there's something else to consider. If you have a producing team of people who are all investing in the film, you're going to want to have investor agreements; again, to avoid misunderstandings and conflict later on. These can be simple and should include, besides name, etc., the amount each person is investing and the recoupment path. You want to make sure that your investors (you) get paid back before any deferments or anything else is paid, plus interest. And then you want to have a clause as to how profits will be divided up based upon each investor's contribution to the film fund. There are tax repercussions that are different depending on whether you have a corporation or a proprietor business but you'll have to talk to your accountant about that.

HOW TO RAISE MONEY

Sometimes you will have struggled to set aside a nest egg that you want to use for your film. Maybe you only have some of it and need to raise the rest. Say you have a budget of $10,000 and you personally only have $2,500. How do you get the rest? Money is hard to come by, it's the scarcest resource there is and we're all struggling to get it together. I'll give you a few suggestions but you will note that none of them include crowdfunding, which I discuss below in the chapter on production. Just briefly, I think your crowdfunding will be more credible and more successful when you have already started shooting your movie. I'll return to this later in more detail.

Get a part-time job or two. If you don't have kids this is easier, of course. Nobody said making your movie would be easy and this is not an unusual method. If you do this, open a separate bank account and put every penny from this job in there so that it's away from temptation and so that you can see it grow, which will inspire you.

Investors. Never had one other than my team so I don't have much to add here. Got a rich uncle or aunt? Maybe you can ask them for some money. Maybe you're a slick salesperson and can convince your dentist to throw a few G's your way. If this is your strategy, then you're probably going to want to create a slick business plan that explains how they will recoup their money (with a clear disclaimer saying that films are a high risk investment and you have no control over the market).

Get your team to buy in. This was what we did. To ease the burden, the four partners in our production company all kicked in money. On our first film production cost us $20K. Five thousand dollars is easier to swallow and pay back than twenty. Our second film ended up being around $7K, mostly because we learned how to do it smarter and thus cheaper. That meant our individual contributions were less than a resort vacation in Jamaica (if that's your thing). On our first film our actor-producers also re-invested their salary into the film, since we were using the ACTRA TIP program and the actors were all paid. However, if their deferred fees were being counted as investment, we made sure that the directors' and writer's fees were also counted as investment, not just as deferment, to be fair. Be careful asking for this, especially if your partners are new friends. We had known our partners for years and had collaborated on other projects before. Diplomacy and good judgment is key here.

Be entrepreneurial. Throw keg parties and charge people for entry. Have bake sales and garage sales. If you're young and have a lot of friends you can make hundreds of dollars at a single kegger. Maybe you're a foodie and love to cook great food. Charge people to come to a banquet prepared by you. Do this sort of thing once a month. Then you're not just asking them for money, you're giving them something of value, so they don't feel like it's charity. And you're bringing them along for the journey and the struggle to make your film. It gives them buy-in, which will also help later with your crowdfunding. Be creative.

Debt. This can be dangerous but if done smart can make all kinds of things possible. On our first film we re-negotiated our mortgage and took out enough equity to cover our portion of the investment total. It wasn't a huge amount so we weren't worried that it was going to cause us to have a major burden in terms of mortgage payments (actually I believe our monthly fees went down though it will be my grandchildren who have to pay off the house). On our second film we had to fix our collapsing front porch and so had gotten a low interest line of credit. Our portion of the contribution was less than $4,000, so we just slopped it onto the LOC and paid it off over the course of a year or so. However, I can't say this enough – don't lose your house over your film. Always remember, it's just a movie and it isn't worth ruining your life. You want to be solvent enough to make a second movie. And a third. Etc.

Probably you will have to do a combination of these things to raise the five or ten or fifteen thousand dollars that you need to make your movie. And if you come up short of what you hoped, then think of ways you can cut back in your film. Do you really need a crane to get that god shot? Can you use a step-ladder instead? Making a nano budget film is all about ingenuity. What's important is that you don't think of this kind of fundraising as degrading or a pain in the butt because it's different from how big films raise capital. Of course it is; you're making a different kind of film.

It's not easy for larger films either. They have to go cap in hand to financiers and funding agencies that aren't interested in building community or even the story, per se. They're interested in numbers on business plans. Their idea of audience building is to attach known quantities (this actor is worth $5 million in this or that market; the sales of this toy indicate that it could be translated into a kids' movie that will move this many units and have the potential for this much merchandising with hats and lunch boxes).

You don't have brand recognition or bankable stars. You have real human beings, networks of support, community and enthusiasm. You need to build on that. It's grassroots and it can be a lot more fun than sitting in meetings with suits who just want to know how you're going to make them money.

CREW

You want to keep your crew as small as possible on a microbudget shoot. Remember, every person on set is somebody else you have to feed – and food will probably be your single largest budget item. You need to be agile and simple. Your focus is story, not on being fancy.

That's going to mean saying "no" sometimes. For instance, your director of photography really, really wants to shoot with some fancy camera that requires a real camera department with several assistant camera people. Don't do it.

I shot once with a DP for a short film and was offered a Red camera to shoot on – this was shortly after they came out and everyone was very excited about them. It seemed like a great idea. But we ended up with a three-person camera department and it made both lighting and camera set-ups complicated. Plus the DP hadn't worked on a Red before so that added more time as she figured how to work with the camera during the shoot. As a result we couldn't make our days and it ruined the short because it was all exterior shooting and we lost our light. Chances are you're not going to have budget to go back and reshoot a bunch of scenes because you weren't able to get them the first time around.

Finding crew you can follow the same methods I suggest above for finding your production team. I would make one more suggestion about finding crew and production team or anybody who's going to be involved in your shoot:

Enthusiasm is more important than experience on a microbudget film shoot.

Of course you want people with experience where possible. But that really experienced director of photography who won't lift a light because that's the gaffer's job will be worse for your film than the less experienced DP who is pumped to get his/her first feature credit and comes with lots of ideas how to improvise. Always trust your gut.

I once had a 1st AD who thought he knew more than me, the director. He probably did. But when we were shooting and he was questioning every single call that I made, shot choices, actor direction, all his experience didn't matter. He was undermining my authority as the director and being a pain in the butt. He was damaging the shoot. You will have enough pains without adding personnel who will be pains as well. If someone starts to become seriously high maintenance or undermines you – get rid of them immediately. At the end of the day though. Don't fire someone in the middle of a shooting day. It could get ugly and cost you the whole day and maybe some other crew. Nobody likes to be around a shitshow when they could be home playing Xbox. And make sure you have a replacement in place. Don't hamstring yourself.

NUMBERS GAME

So, what is the perfect number of people for a microbudget shoot and what positions should you fill? It depends. If you have a budget of $5000 you will have different needs and resources than if you're shooting for $50,000. But I think there's some guidelines for what you must have. I think that you want to have an organizer on set to keep things together that aren't director responsibilities – a production manager and a 1st AD. On our first film, *A Brand New You* we had both *and* a 2nd AD. On *Fucking My Way Back Home* we had just a PM/1st AD in a combined role and no 2nd AD to wrangle cast. If you're the producer you can play this role or get a PA to help out.

Unless you're shooting yourself you will want a DP, who will also probably be the camera operator. I'd personally recommend having a separate DP so that the director can focus on being a director. We also had a "swing" on both of our films who was both gaffer and grip. We could have used a PA for this job but having someone who knew lighting, knew how to keep cables safe and to keep track of gear was really useful and saved us time and headaches. And, for goodness sakes, have a sound person. I know that some people say "oh, get the PA to hold the boom" or have the director hold the boom. But an audio recordist is more than just a person holding a boom mic. They are entirely focused on getting good sound. They are managing probably a boom and several LAV mics running through a mixer. They are listening to whether there were background noises that were audible during the take, like a plane flying overhead or a car horn in the distance. This can kill you in post-production. I know of a film that didn't have a proper sound kit and a dedicated audio recordist and they had to ADR – have actors re-record their lines in the studio – *every single line of dialogue* in the movie afterwards. The movie was good but it was like watching an old Godzilla movie dubbed from Japanese, where the lips and the words were never quite in synch.

On both of our films we had both a hair & make-up artist (MUA) and a wardrobe person. This can be combined and simplified but there's a danger that they will mess up continuity if there's changes in wardrobe, etc. and you're shooting out of sequence. I think it's worth the extra person to feed to have two people. You will probably have to pay the make-up person for their kit, which is entirely reasonable. We paid $500 to our MUA on both shoots to cover the costs of the make-up and hair product that they used.

To keep wardrobe costs down, where actors couldn't supply from their own wardrobe, our wardrobe person would buy clothes from big chain stores, like H&M and then we would return the clothes later. I don't recommend, as some others do, having your actors do their own make-up. They aren't always the best judge of what kind of make-up looks best on them in particular lighting, etc. They don't have an objective distance that is needed. Do you really want your actor looking as orange as Donald Trump? And your MUA will take photos of actors before their scenes, for continuity later on, and keep track of them.

I read in a recent article on crew sizes that having a script supervisor/continuity person was totally unnecessary because editors never read their notes anyway. I don't know if that's true but they can be a big help on set. The script supervisor on *Fucking My Way Back Home (FMWBH)* saved our bacon more than once. Especially when you're tired or in a rush to get all your shots in, you can miss important details that will cause your film to not make sense. They are there to keep track of all the details of the story big and small. Was that phone on the left hand side of the desk in the reverse angle or the right? These lines of dialogue contradict something that the actor said earlier. We were moving around a lot, shooting in a car in numerous locations, and mostly at night, so we were tired. We shot an entire scene then realized we'd mixed up scene numbers and that scene should have been shot in the heroine's kitchen, not in a car wash. I know, it sounds like a stupid, obvious mistake. Not so much when it's 4am and you're 9 hours into your shoot day. If not for our continuity person we would have had to go back and re-shoot that scene. Finally, they also note which take you preferred. Usually editors will assume that your last take was your favorite, which is why you didn't do more takes. Except that sometimes you get your take and have a bit of extra time and try something different. Maybe your actor has an idea of what might work better. But it doesn't. You want to note the take that you preferred. Our continuity person communicated these details with our editor at the end of each shoot day as we delivered our footage to her. That was one less thing that my co-director and I had to do.

You may think that because you have no budget you're just going to use whatever's in the location for your set-design. Don't kid yourself. When you break down your script there's going to be lots of little items that you will mark out as being needed, from cellphones to pencils to prop knives. There will be pieces of art on location that you will need to cover up unless you have image releases from the creators, brand names to cover up, etc. You might need a lamp or a clock or to deal with some color problems on your set. And someone will need to keep track of all these things. This is both a creative and organizational role. Our Production Designer couldn't be on set many of the nights for our second film and it created hassles. But luckily he was very organized and left us boxes of stuff for every shoot day and every location with everything labeled inside.

I'll talk about this more later but make sure that you have a unit photographer on-set to get publicity shots or you will kick yourself later. You can't re-stage behind the scenes shots and you will need production stills for publicity, for your movie poster, etc. If you can't get someone to be there every day then try to pick strategically which days have the most important scenes.

Lastly, you will need some PA's on-set to help fill the gaps. You might need a PA who can drive when you have unit moves. And a PA to work your craft services. Another to help load and unload gear. There's a lot of little things and big things that don't fit into other roles and for these it's good to have two or three PAs around. We had a dedicated craft food services person on both of our films because keeping people well-fed is extremely important – both for meals and for a snack table.

To summarize, you're looking at:
Director
Production Manager/1st AD
DP
Swing
Sound
Hair & Make-Up Artist
Wardrobe
Production Designer/Set Decorator/Prop Master
Continuity/Script Supervisor
Unit Photographer
2 or 3 PAs

Not including cast, that means you could easily have 14-15 people on set at any given time. That's tiny compared to most films, even ultra low budget ones, but it's still a lot of people to feed and keep track of (thus the need for a PM/1st AD). You can consider merging some of these roles – your DP and your swing, for instance – but just take note of the dangers/extra hassles that this can cause, as I've noted above. Some people like to go uber-guerilla and have a crew as small as three – as Gareth Edwards did when he shot the incredible sci-fi film *Monsters* in Central America for $15,000 (with post it ended up being a lot more than that, with a listed budget of $500,000). It's worth checking out the many videos online about how he did it. I'd personally rather feed people – which you can do for under $10/person/day – than have a panic attack during or after a shoot. And, of course, as your budget grows you can scale up the size of your crew from there. We had this basic set-up for *FMWBH*, which we shot for around $7,000 (Canadian).

CAST

If at all possible, use professional actors at least in your lead roles. There are programs through SAG and ACTRA (in Canada) for ultra-low budget films that allow you to pay a reduced fee, though – at least with ACTRA - it means that all your actors have to be paid and union members (unless you do like Edwards in *Monsters* and shoot out of the country, using non-actors in all your supporting roles). On our last film we used the Co-Op Film program through ACTRA, which meant actors got a percentage of any future profits in lieu of pay, based upon the hours worked. It was an extra hassle to work out everyone's percentage but it saved us thousands of dollars.

I know Mike Leigh uses non-actors in all his roles and makes great movies. You're not Mike Leigh, don't have his budgets and don't have the time to really work on set with your non-actors to get a decent performance if they freeze up, are flat or over-act. You probably only have two or three weeks to shoot your 70-90 page feature film, so you want people who know what they're doing. Here's some benefits to using pro-actors:

They know how to build characters and find motivation and arc. They will become your collaborators in creating the best film possible. They will be able to feel when a line isn't working and help you fix it. And, when you don't have time for tons of takes they will give you better performances.

They know how to act in front of a camera so that you can edit it together later. If your actor moves their body or hands or hair differently in every single take – in one angle they scratch their face, in another they don't, in a third they do something else – you will have a very difficult time cutting together your different shots. They understand a million other technical things about acting on camera, from blinking to eye-lines to finding their marks.

They can act.

Of course you can't always find professional film actors. There are certainly good actors who aren't in the union (and bad ones in the union). But I would suggest that if you use non-professional actors you should add extra time in your schedule because you will probably have to coach them to get the performance you need. Again, as with crew size, you have to find the balance that you're comfortable with between going guerilla and covering your bases, which takes more money and organization.

AUDITIONS

Maybe, like us, you have two or three actor friends with whom you want to work. That reduces your need to audition, though likely there will still be a few roles to fill. You can post audition notices on Craigslist or through union job boards. There's also great paid services, like castingworkbook.com, where you can find oodles of great actors. We held auditions for our first film in a bar that we could get for free. It had space for us to set up, tables that we could use to sit behind and watch the performance, a waiting area if an actor showed up early, etc. For our second film we used actors whom we knew and trusted and so didn't hold any auditions.

You probably know the look you're going for but when you start getting headshots and reels, keep an open mind. Consider trying more than one type for your roles. Try with type, against type, something unexpected. Sometimes you can be surprised and really enrich a role "by accident".

Here's a few tips to running auditions:

Schedule people 15-20 minutes apart so you have time to play a bit and time to make a few notes after they're done.

Video the auditions so that you can go back to them later if you need to.

Send them "sides" to rehearse before the audition. You want to see how they interpret the role in that scene. Actors also do best when they feel prepared. But don't expect them to be "off book". They might have multiple auditions that day.

Give them one or two directions: "play it angrier", "try it sitting down/standing up", "deliver your lines in a whisper". You want to see how well they take direction and if they can be flexible. Feel free to steal stuff from previous actors – someone played it quiet and menacing and that choice interested you. How does this actor work with that choice?

Give them another short scene to read cold to see how they do under pressure.

Thank them when they arrive, tell them that they did a really great job and thank them for coming. Auditions suck for actors and it's a hard job. Make them feel good about what they did.

INTERVIEW WITH AN ACTOR

Manuel Rodriguez-Saenz starred in both *A Brand New You* **and** *Fucking My Way Back Home.* **He has been an actor and a clown for almost 20 years and has had roles in larger budget productions and television, including Ricky Gervais'** *Special Correspondents.*

What did you find most different about acting in a no-budget film?

I think resources is the most obvious difference, it doesn't necessarily compromise quality but the comfort level of having big crews with several people in several departments, more prep and shooting time, etc. changes the approach and roles for everyone on set and the actors are not an exception from these dynamics. On a "regular" set as an actor you'll have lots of people attending to you, a private trailer, mostly everything is delivered to you and your only focus is on your character, lines and the next scene.

Comfortably waiting in your trailer to be called to set is a luxury that a no-budget film can't afford, not just from a financial point of view. You're also assisting other crew and being there to help as needed. It's not that as an actor you are not given the chance to work on your craft. But in a no-budget film the pace is much faster. There's also the creative freedom that as an actor you don't have as much on a regular set. [In a regular budget film] you don't have much say about your wardrobe, character traits, actions. But in a no-budget innovation and creativity are a must and you get to be more in control of your craft.

Was your prep different in any way?
The main thing to get used to is the fast pace of the shoot. You end up doing the same type of prep that you would normally do but you have to be able to access your emotions faster and a good way of helping me with that while doing my prep was having "key words" or images to remind me the premises or emotions involved in the scene.

What was your biggest challenge and what was/would have been most useful for you in that setting?
Not to have a break in the middle of the shoot [on *A Brand New You*]. Shooting for twelve days straight while trying to balance life and fight physical and emotional exhaustion. Some time off would be prudent.

Do you have one piece of advice for microbudget filmmakers making a feature?
Use professional actors, committed to their craft. Not only will help to save time but a trained actor will be ready for any sudden changes and give you peace of mind during the chaos that can be shooting a low budget movie

5 PRIOR PLANNING PREVENTS POOR PERFORMANCE

It's important to say that a lot of this stuff you will be doing simultaneously once you have your producing team in place. You will be finding crew and cast as you make your plans and get your gear and raise the last of your budget. But it's now that we turn to the planning process. Any film requires solid planning because even the simplest no budget film is going to have a lot of moving parts. There's a lot of improvising that has to happen on a microbudget. It will often feel like you're running on sand against a windstorm. Nothing feels secure. But the better your pre-production planning, the more you will be able to improvise when the inevitable crises hit.

BREAK IT DOWN

You will almost certainly be making changes to your script right up till the day production starts. And even after, on the fly, on-set, you will make adjustments as you realize there are holes in your bullet-proof script, or that a section of dialogue just isn't working. But you still want to have the best script possible, a production draft, and then you want to break it down. There are 2 major parts to breaking down the script.

SCHEDULING

Shooting a film in sequence is a nice idea but for the sake of efficiency it almost never works. Even still, you want to have a very detailed script breakdown and schedule so that you know each and every day what you will be shooting, what you will need for those days in terms of props, costumes, cast, equipment etc. This is finicky work but it will save your life and your film on set. I would say that most of the time this is even true if you are improvising a lot of the script. You still want to know when you will be shooting what to make sure that you shoot your beginning, middle and end and don't end up with any holes in your story.

There are programs out there that automate a lot of the scheduling process – though it's still tedious, detail-oriented work. Movie Magic Scheduling is $185 (the "Pro" version is about three times that) though you can subscribe to Celtx' scheduling software for $10/month. On *ABNY* our poor 1st AD did it all in an Excel spreadsheet and it was hellish. On *FMWBH* we got a copy of Movie Magic and it made the process a million times easier. Whatever direction you go, here are the basic tasks:

The first thing you need to do is create scene breakdown sheets. You will have to go through your script scene by scene and underline all the different breakdown elements. If you're using Final Draft or the free script software Celtx, they have built-in "tagging" that allows you to select and mark these items for loading later into scheduling software and saves a lot of typing. The first thing is that you will have to number all of your scenes, easy to select in Final Draft and Celtx, and create separate sheets for each scene. On each breakdown sheet you will need the following information:

Scene number and name/short summary – "Paul confronts Mary about her infidelity"

Setting – "Paul's House"

Location – "39 Main St, 2nd floor"

Whether it is Day or Night, Interior or Exterior.

The number of pages that scene occupies, divided by eighths of a page. So, like 1 2/8, 2 1/8, etc.

The characters who appear in that scene

Any special equipment needed – greenscreen, for instance, or steadicam

All the props in that scene

Any special hair, make-up or wardrobe elements

Any sound or light effects

Any "stunts", like a fist fight

If you're doing it manually – and probably even if you're not – use a series of different colored pencils for each element. So, underline your characters in red, your props in blue, etc. There are industry standard colors but these aren't as important as just consistently using the same color. You'll want to go through the script twice to make sure that your eyes weren't glazing over with boredom and you missed something. Then you will either use the tagger function, if you have scheduling software, or you will create a breakdown template sheet and input all the elements. Make copies of your breakdown sheets and then put them in binders for your heads of department who will use this for their own planning. These are incredibly important and will be referenced frequently by everyone on set, from make-up to the 1st AD who is making up call sheets for each day (one of the bonuses of using Movie Magic is that it will generate all your reports for you).

STRIP IT

The other important thing that the breakdown sheets make possible is your scheduling. You want to make sure you shoot your entire film and don't end up with 20 pages left to shoot at the end. "Making your day" is one of the key jobs of any director, that is shooting all the scenes that you have scheduled. Knowing your schedule will discipline you, and if you aren't disciplined, it will allow your 1st AD to bully you into being disciplined.

Your schedule is called a stripboard and was traditionally made up of a whole whack of strips of paper with some key information on them that would get moved around in relation to each other in order to schedule your shoot. Again, scheduling software like Movie Magic or Celtx will automatically generate these strips. These strips will allow you to know what scenes you're shooting each day, do it in a rational way that maximizes efficiency and makes sure that you don't have some days that are impossibly long and other days that are pointlessly short.

Never, ever plan for 16-hour days. It may seem like a smart way to get your shoot done in two weeks instead of three or one week instead of two but it kills your crew and cast. Performances drop in quality. Things get broken. Crew stop turning up to set because your shoot sucks to work on, or they get sick. Cast lose their voices. You name it. We tried to keep to 10-hour days knowing that sometimes we would go over but it kept us to less than 12-hours.

Here's some principles to apply in your scheduling.

Schedule exterior scenes first in your production schedule. If there is bad weather it allows you to move up an interior day and shoot your exterior day later in your shoot when the weather has improved.

Keep together your night shoots and your day shoots so that you don't for example, have your crew up all night and then starting at 7am the next day.

Try to keep the number of pages you're shooting on any given day roughly equal to other days. On our first feature we shot 8-12 pages per day and on our second we shot about 6 per day but we moved around a lot more, shot in a moving car, etc.

Start soft. Make your first couple of days lighter as people get used to working together. Don't schedule really heavy emotional scenes or any action scenes in your first few days. Let people warm up.

Be aware that scenes with a lot of action will take longer to shoot than dialogue scenes where you will probably shoot from less angles, requiring less lighting set-ups, etc. (we generally were able to do about 30 set-ups per day with very simple lighting needs). Take that into account and give them more time. Ditto any complicated shooting that you have planned – shooting handheld or on a tripod is quicker than using a steadicam or a dolly shot, which requires extra prep time. That really cool drone shot of the car driving away is going to take a lot longer than you think. If you're not sure, ask the crew responsible how long they think they'll need and then double it.

Try to keep your actors' days together. Sometimes, if you're paying professionals, this can save you money as the union may demand that you book actors for the days around a call day. It's also just considerate to an actor who has to take time off of other work, rather than booking them for two days one week, one day the next and three days on the third. Doing that can make them unavailable for other jobs on all those weeks.

Use scheduling to save money on food. If you only need an actor for half a day, put it all in the morning or after lunch so that you don't have to feed them a full meal.

COUNT IT

Just as with scheduling, you want your budget to be as planned out as possible. Some things will be easier to know the cost of than others, especially when you don't have experience shooting a feature. But you know how much money you have to spend. You don't want to get two-thirds of the way into a shoot and suddenly run out of money or realize that you need to come up with 50% more cash to cover the final days. Sticking to budget prevents broken hearts and broken marriages. Make this as real as possible.

If you're hiring actors through union agreements you will know in advance exactly what your costs will be in this area. Ditto if you're paying anyone else. If you're paying your actors $5000 and your budget is $12,000 that needs to be divided up between the different departments. Food will be your next big budget item. On a film that typically has 10-15 people for lunch every day you could spend over $1000, depending on how you get your food (more on this later). Does your DP need to rent any lenses or buy any consummables, like filters or tape? How many lights are you going to use? How much will your sound gear cost? Take the time to price this out and put it into your budget in Excel. The more accurately you know the price of things, the more you can make strategic decisions – "the gorilla suit isn't THAT important but we really need those high quality LAV mics because we have a lot of outdoor shots". Try to set aside a contingency fund of five or ten percent of your total budget to cover any unexpected expenses, like someone parks a production vehicle in front of a fire hydrant.

GEAR IT

Sometimes gear will come with crew – DP's often have some lights and gels, for instance and will provide these free or at a low cost rental to cover depreciation. Maybe they have a handheld rig, a camera and a tripod. Your sound person might work for free but charge you to rent their gear (this is what we did on our first film). Your make-up artist has their own kit and will just charge you a kit fee – we paid $500 on both films to cover the use of our MUA's kit. Here's some other tips for getting stuff for cheap or free:

You can use actors' clothing or buy stuff and then return it after the shoot (thank you H&M for making our film possible).

If you have an IKEA nearby they also have a very liberal returns policy. You can practically furnish entire homes with the stuff and then bring it back – undamaged – later, no questions asked. Ditto Walmart. Free production design!

Buy it then re-sell it instead of renting. God love e-Bay. On our first film we bought our three point video lighting set-up on e-Bay for $200 and sold it later for basically the same amount, minus the cost of shipping. On our second shoot we bought high quality sound gear with a high resale value on e-Bay and then re-sold it afterwards on e-Bay for a profit. In general I would recommend buying used – far in advance, to make sure it works. This is because the devaluation of previous ownership has already happened and is reflected in a cheaper price. You're only using it for another two or three weeks so it's not like the price should go down even further. As soon as something is used it immediately drops in price for resale. Sometimes by a lot.

Barter can sometimes work. Through our PM we knew a guy with a videography company who wanted to accumulate producing credits. He let us use his DJI Ronin and some other gear for nothing in return for a credit for his production company.

When you think about gearing up, think about your locations. We shot in a car for a lot of *FMWBH* and that meant no access to power. A generator would have been too loud (and too expensive). So we used LED lights running on batteries because LEDs use very little power compared to other types of lights. They were also cheap ($150 for each Polaroid lighting bank on Amazon) and we re-sold them afterwards.

Make a list of everything that you need and price it out – on Amazon, eBay, whatever – assume that it will cost you 25% more than what you calculate for the initial purchase (there's always surprises with shipping, taxes, duties, didn't come with a spare battery or bulbs, etc). Then assume that you can re-sell half the purchased gear for 75% of the initial price. Put those numbers into your budget. If they push you over the top, go back and trim what you "need." If you come in under budget, good. You probably won't in the real world. Or another area will come in over budget and you can use surplus from your gear budget.

As an addendum to all this, I would seriously consider getting production insurance. We have for both of our productions. It's a few hundred bucks and covers you if the house you're shooting in goes up in flames and you lose everything. It also provides liability insurance if anyone is hurt on set. As with everything there is a risk/cost calculation but this was a risk we didn't want to take.

LIST IT

In sticking with the motto of being as well planned as possible, you really ought to create shot lists for all of your scenes. I would also take the time to draw out blocking & camera diagrams for your shots as well. On our first film we did these by hand. On our second we used an iPad app called Shot Designer by the people who created the video course called *Hollywood Camera Work*. It allows you to create comprehensive diagrams, including movement, camera and lighting set-ups, etc. You can get pretty fancy but its a bit complicated to get the hang of at first and sometimes on set I found it confusing to remember what I had intended with all the overlaid shots. But that might have just been me.

An important point about shot lists: Make sure you list and plan to get meat and potatoes shots first. You are on a tight schedule and fancy shots can take up a lot of time. It's nice to have a few of these sprinkled throughout your film but its more important that you get enough coverage to be able to cut together a coherent scene at the end, even if it's the old standard – medium- close-up shot-reverse close-up. Put in some bonus shots that you can always try for if you finish the meat and potatoes first. And ALWAYS get cutaways – shots of key objects, the character's fidgeting hands, the dog sleeping in the corner. You'd be surprised how often you will use these in editing; to control pacing, to cover-up a camera dropping out of focus on your one otherwise good take, etc.

In general, but especially if you have action, it's useful to visit your locations and map out your blocking. This will change on set (everything will change on set) but it gives you a more realistic sense of how people and gear can move in a space. Expect, where you have action involving more than two people that you will need more angles than you think. If possible visit first and make diagrams. Then bring your DP with you to the locations. They will have ideas and will help you avoid "crossing the line". You can also map out on your diagrams with them things like lighting to save consultation time on set when you have a dozen people standing around. You want to shoot a lot of improvised action? It's ironic but the better is your planning, the more room you will have for improvisation.

LOCATE IT

Unless you're making a horror movie (or a porn, I suppose) you're probably going to have more than one location. Avoid big institutional settings because they're expensive. Unless you know someone who owns or managers a big institution and can get you in free. And try to cheat locations – like using different rooms or spaces in the same location as though they are different locations entirely and then shoot an establishing shot of a different building. Film is magical that way.

But for any location that you shoot you're going to want to scout it with your department heads. Your production designer will want to talk about dressing the set and it will be helpful to see it. They'll also want to see what brands they may have to cover, including copyrighted images like a painting or photograph (you don't want to have to pay to cover up all that stuff in post, which is way more expensive). They can do this cheaply with fancy wrapping paper (really). In Toronto there's a store called The Japanese Paper Place where you can get beautiful, handmade paper. It's not copyrighted and it looks great in a frame. Your PD will want to know how many prints are on the wall so that they don't all have the same designed paper and want to know what colors they need. Your wardrobe person will have thoughts about what colors will look good there. Your DP will want to see what options are available for rigging lighting and you will want to block it out with them, etc. You don't want to discover on the day that there aren't enough outlets and not have a mini-generator (we bought a couple of car battery boosters for $100. They're cheap and silent and you can charge one while using the other to recharge your spare camera batteries, laptop, lighting batteries, etc.)

You also want to get the owner of the location, even if it's you, to sign a location agreement allowing you to use the space for the designated dates and to have the rights to use images taken of the space. That will be important as part of your deliverables if you want to get distribution for your film. When you're done shooting, make sure you get the owner to sign a location release confirming that you've done no damage to the space and have left it as you found it.

If you're using exterior, street locations your city will want you to have shooting permits. Whether you get them or not is up to you but if you have production insurance they are pretty easy to get through your city's film office (every big city almost certainly has one). They're generally very helpful and will tell you exactly what you need to do, whether it's get permission from the neighbors, etc.

We did a mix of shooting guerilla style and having permits. For instance, we were towing around a car with our actors inside. Technically that's illegal and you're supposed to have a paid duty officer, directing traffic, collecting overtime, etc. We didn't get one of those but instead told them that we'd be doing short shoots in several locations and got a roaming permit for that. If we were pulled over we would have told them that we were in transit to the next location and didn't know we couldn't have the actors in the vehicle being towed. We never had a problem and were only questioned by a cop once while shooting a stationary shot at the side of a downtown street. He gave us a bit of a hard time but our papers were in order so he couldn't fine us or send us on our way.

FEED IT

There's another kind of list that you want to make before you go to camera: your menu. You can't afford a craft truck so... you are the craft truck. Sometimes you can get food donated by local businesses, restaurants, or dad but don't count on it. And, even if you do, you will still need a well-planned menu.

Schedule meals for every single day – you will need two meals plus snacks and drinks. Assign meals to people on the production team and start cooking and freezing a few weeks in advance. If you're shooting five days a week for three weeks, you don't need 15 different meals. Come up with five dishes, make triple what you need for any given day and then freeze it in three batches. Assign a PA, or rotate your PAs so that they don't feel stuck in the kitchen the whole shoot, and make sure you have enough servings to cover everyone. Send a PA or two out at the beginning of each day to buy snacks at the grocery store (after they put on a big pot of coffee) based upon the number of people on set that day. Don't forget to calculate in bottled water, plastic cups, plates, etc. DON'T SERVE PIZZA. Crews make jokes about shoots that serve pizza because it's tacky. The other thing is that you really want to avoid serving high carb meals because it makes everyone sleepy and sluggish afterwards. It's worth the extra money to keep your crew fed with tasty, high quality, high protein meals. They will like you more and, more importantly, they will perform better. It's worth the $1.50/person/day. Finally, make sure that every day at ever location there is a well-stocked snack table with healthy snacks – fruit, veggies, beef jerky, coffee and tea, cold water, muffins in the morning.

It's also best to send out a questionnaire to cast and crew beforehand to see if there's any food allergies. Or just do what we did – always have a vegetarian version available for a few people and avoid the most common allergy culprits – no nuts, no gluten, no dairy.

MARKET IT

It may seem strange to think about this now but building excitement for your film starts well before you go to camera. You want everyone you know to know that you're making a movie and you want them to be excited about it. Hollywood has made filmmaking seem more glamorous than it really is.

People love to hear about how you're doing it, they love photos and short videos. And this can start during pre-production.

Set-up a Facebook page and start inviting everyone on the planet to "like" it. Set up a blog and post stuff from it on a regular basis. Consider also setting up a Twitter and Instagram account. Set up integration so that your Instagram posts will automatically post to Facebook and your Facebook posts will automatically post to Twitter, etc.

Go to fiverr.com and pay a designer five bucks to make you a quick movie logo, even if you don't use it later. Seriously. Unless you're a designer yourself, that five bucks will get you a better logo than you can create in two hours in your crappy design program. You can use this across your social media properties.

Start a blog detailing your experience. During pre-production this will probably be once a week or less. During production, even though you're exhausted at the end of every day, take 10 minutes to write up the one thing that you learned while shooting that day or the one unexpected thing that happened. Upload pictures.

While I have said elsewhere that you should write your passion, it is worth considering whether your passion connects with a niche audience. This can help your film get a wider reach. If so you can target your marketing to attract interest by posting material that engages with this audience, whether it be dog breeders, people of a particular religious affiliation or those who have a particular social concern. You can spend five bucks a day to create Facebook ads to promote your page to this niche audience. Creating Facebook ads is super-easy and it can actually work, that's why Zuckerberg is so rich. Forget Google Ads, you need a PhD to figure out how to use it. We'll discuss this more in the section on distribution strategies.

Make sure that you have an on-set photographer or two – and a videographer if you can get one at least for some days – to come and shoot stills and behind the scenes material (known as extra-diagetic content). You will need this to enter festivals, which want stills. And if you ever try to sell your film to a distributor you will have to have stills. You will also need them for your movie poster.

If you can, find a marketing intern from a local college who will bottom-line all this – or an enthusiastic member of your production team. You can also find social media marketing interns on Craigslist. They can schedule posts, solicit material, come on set and film short smartphone interviews with you, your cast and crew. If there's a niche for your film you can set up a Google notification that will send you articles related to that subject every time something is posted on the interwebs. You can then re-post this stuff, which will interest your audience, on your Facebook page. This material that you're generating will also be useful when you run your crowdfunding campaign for post-production funds (we'll get to that). Having a marketer means its one less thing for you to have to think of that isn't directly related to making the movie. There's even a name for this position, coined by the indie documentary filmmaker John Reiss – Producer of Marketing & Distribution. Put this person on your production team. That's how important they are – they have a producer title. Then when you write your production diary you can just email it to them to post and promote along with your snazzy photos.

CRECHE IT

One of the (many) barriers to women in film is the lack of childcare. My wife and I co-direct and we have two kids so I am painfully aware of the challenges of childcare while shooting a film. You should be aware of this too. We provided money for babysitting to actors/actresses who had kids. And would have done for other crew if it was necessary. This, like providing high quality food for your unpaid crew, is the decent thing to do.

But we also had to worry about our own childcare as we were on-set 10-12 hours a day. For our daytime shoots this wasn't such a huge deal as we had a childcare provider, though we had to fill some holes and we had friends and family provide this. For our second feature, it was mostly shot at night. We really leaned on friends with kids to come and have sleepovers with their kid at our house (our youngest was still too young to sleep at someone else's house). And my mother-in-law took our kids for one of the three weeks.

You can also be creative and organize childcare relatively cheaply but you have to plan it in advance, whether it's booking an ECE/nanny for daytime to look after several kids or having someone come and sleep over. Put this on your producing team to-do list. You're making a microbudget movie because you have stories that you don't think should be excluded from cinema just because you lack connections, riches, experience, etc. It's good for your karma if you treat cast and crew with kids in the same way – ie. facilitating their voice getting into cinema.

INTERVIEW WITH A PRODUCTION MANAGER

Holly Rowden was the Production Manager and 1st AD on *Fucking My Way Back Home* **and has also produced a number of short films. At the time of this interview she was a recent graduate from the film program at Humber College in Toronto, Canada.**

What is most difficult about shooting a microbudget feature for a PM and 1st AD

One of the most difficult things was the fact that I was both the PM and the 1st AD. This put me in charge of scheduling and running the set, as well as dealing with permits, petty cash, and transportation. I found myself unable to fufill both duties fully, with one of the two sets of responsibilities suffering while I prioritized the other. Never had I experienced an inability to do the job fully due to a lack of *time* in my life. There were not enough minutes in the day.

The production definitely went over time where we could. This is natural working with inexperienced crew (I include myself here), and with limited resources, it's difficult to plan for things that go wrong. For example, I recall scheduling a shoot day with nine pages, simply because we had no other days on which we could shoot the scene. That being said, we all knew what we were signing up for, or at least I hope that we did!

With a microbudget, where no one is getting paid, everyone is doing the job on the side, in addition to whatever responsibilities they may have in their everyday lives. It's tough to work around everyone's schedules, and cater to their other commitments. For instance, instead of having one makeup artist, we had to change daily in order to respect their two work schedules. Some people would call me last minute and tell me that they couldn't make it due to one reason or another. And though it sucks, there isn't really a lot you can do about it.

What was your biggest challenge shooting a microbudget feature

Working on a set where no one was getting paid, I found it really difficult to be a hardass. On the one hand, it's my job to make sure that everyone is on task. This sometimes requires me to be more aggressive with crew than I would like. On the other hand, these people aren't getting paid. Perhaps my personality is not cut out to be an AD, but I did find it most helpful to assist in problem solving, looking for ways to help the production increase efficiency, rather than bark out orders to crew.

What did you enjoy most?

Everyday I felt I was learning something new. Be it a tough lesson, like getting stuck in the rain, or an easy one, it's a great feeling to walk away feeling like you have gained something from the experience. I learned more on this feature than any paid gig I have ever had. Microbudgets give you the opportunity to work with more responsibility than you would normally have.

It was an incredibly busy shoot, and I'm sure everyone was underslept. To know that, at the end of the day, your blood sweat and tears is going into the foundation of a piece of art is incredibly satisfying. I know that the final product was worth it to me.

How can directors on microbudgets work more effectively with a PM and 1st AD to get the best possible work?

On any film, there are going to be compromises, and ever more so on a microbudget. I felt that many sacrifices were made on this film for the sake of scheduling, money, and locations. This is all a part of the process, but having a director who is ready to compromise on some things means you'll walk away with the most usable content.

In addition to this, a constant flow of communication is absolutely vital to the success of the shoot. It's the PM and AD's job to be aware of and master all the different working parts of the set. This includes the director's vision. They must know what the director wants so that they can best organize the crew, schedule, budget, etc. to facilitate that vision.

Any other advice for PMs, producers, ADS of filmmakers more generally thinking of making a microbudget?

Stay positive. Like I said, at the end of the day, you're not doing it for the money, or the fame. You're doing it to learn something, and hopefully make something meaningful in the process. Other crew look to the PMs, ADs, directors and producers for guidance. You are responsible for creating a positive and open environment. You set the standards for hard work and positivity.

6 THESE BOOTS WERE MADE FOR WALKING

You've got a great script. You've done all your pre-production work and you're as organized as you can be. Your film is cast and your crew is in place and you've got all the necessary gear. You've met with your department heads (who are probably also the department) both individually and then as a group to answer any questions, give the battle plan and inspire the troops for the tough slog that lies ahead. Now you're ready to go to camera.

HOME BASE

You're going to need a production office that will be your home base. We used our house on the first feature and the lead actor's apartment on the second. We had our meals there and we stored all our crew and our documents there (on the second shoot our PM took the paperwork home with her each day). It's a hassle to have all that stuff in your home but on the plus side it's free and you can sleep with your hard drives in your bed if you're anxious about your footage. Get some shelving – either clear off space, buy a unit from IKEA or, if you're handy, build something simple.

At the end of every day make sure your department heads inventory absolutely everything and put it in its slot. In the chaos of any shoot, but perhaps even more in a no budget shoot where people wear multiple hats, it's easy for stuff to get mixed up and misplaced. Better you run around looking for lens caps and batteries at the end of the day when you've released your actors and there's nothing else to shoot than at the beginning of the day when everyone is waiting. Remember to keep the boxes if you purchased any gear for when you re-sell it.

Especially if you're married and have a spouse who, up to now, has been tolerant of your filmmaking dreams, make sure that you and/or people on your team do the dishes and clean up at the end of every day. You want to make sure all this stuff is organized as well, in its own boxes and/or shelves. We know from experience how quickly things can get chaotic. Our house was the production office AND the main set in our first film. Our bedroom was the hair, make-up and wardrobe room so we woke up staring at costumes and hair irons for two weeks straight.

At the end of every day you also want to organize your footage and keep back-ups off-site, just in case. We would make one back-up of our footage that would be dropped off at our editor's house, a second that the DP would take home and archive on Blu-Ray discs and the original was kept in our production office. Luckily hard drive storage has come down a lot in price so we had two large storage drives (3TB), plus a few smaller drives for transferring footage to our editor each day (she would send back the previous day's drive after she had transferred it to her own large drive. We mostly only needed two drives for these transfers but we had one extra just in case the person dropping off the new drive didn't pick-up the previous drive.

KISS THIS

I had an annoying teacher when I was a kid who would always say: Keep it simple, stupid (KISS). Unfortunately for me I like complexity and made my life more difficult to spite him. But you're a microbudget film production and there's no room to get crazy. If there's an overall rule, besides being very organized, I would say it is this. Here's ten tips to surviving your production:

Keep lighting set-ups simple where possible and be prepared to resist a DP who is a perfectionist, unless you're planning on shooting on weekends spread out over months and so aren't worried about time. If, like us, you're going to shoot 30 set-ups a day, there's not a lot of time to get fancy. Luckily, the sensors in DSLRs and video cameras have come a long way and you can shoot great stuff with minimal light. For our in-car night shots we used two Polaroid LED panels that cost us $150/each (re-sold for $100 each).

Focus on meat and potato shots to get your coverage but spread some "money shots" throughout the film to add some production value. Handheld can add dynamism to a shot if your DP or camera operator has a steady hand. But there's other possibilities too. The DP on our first film was a bit of a daredevil doc filmmaker and sat on the trunk of a slow moving car to shoot our hero riding his bicycle for an opening shot (note: don't kill anyone to get a shot). Get some exterior shots to cut back on the claustrophobia of shooting in more easily controlled interiors, typical of microbudgets. For our second film we shot a lot in a car that was being towed by a pick-up truck. We rented both privately, including the trailer, which we found on Craigslist for $250 (UHaul would have cost us around

$1,000). You'd be amazed what you can rent on Craigslist. It's a great resource.

In addition to a shot list its useful to have some alternative performances you'd like to get from your actors so that you have variety in the editing room. You may not have the time to try these and you may have to rely on the ability of your actors to know their characters once you've given them their blocking and clarified the goal of the scene. But it's good to have in case of extra time.

If possible have an assistant editor/editor on-set or nearby to log and organize your footage while you shoot. We never had time to watch dailies between the day of shooting and having to take care of our kids. I don't believe in ruining marriages or giving your kids abandonment issues in order to shoot a movie. But we did want to know that there weren't technical issues.

Make your days. This is really important. You don't have resources to extend your shooting and if possible you want to avoid having to shoot pick-ups at a later date for anything other than some b-roll or establishing shots. The last thing you want is to only have half your script in the can. I story edited a wonderful script on a two million dollar movie. Best script I'd read that year. The film is a one star film, mainly because the director only shot two-thirds of the script and the film barely makes sense.

Be Flexible I: You're shooting on a really tight schedule. You're probably going to find yourself running behind sometimes. Your AD/PM will come up to you during lunch to have a conversation and want to know what to do. You will have to make decisions on the fly about what not to shoot. Cut transition scenes, not core scenes; things like your character getting from one place to another. Remember, it's easier to shoot establishing shots of a location or even of characters MOS, than it is to shoot a complex scene with sound, lighting, etc. On both of our films we shot some MOS pick-ups that required a crew of us plus our DP (on the first we needed a make-up artist as well).

Be Flexible II: Things come up. Our annoying rock n roll neighbors decided to have a backyard concert while we were shooting our first film. We had permits and they didn't. We could have fought with them and maybe called the cops. Instead we made a compromise – we would start our day an hour earlier and they would start theirs an hour later. And they would let us shoot our leads going to their concert. What could have been a crisis turned out to be a really nice little montage that deepened the relationship between our leads. We also made compromises on some locations and ended up with stuff that was better than our original plan. Think in terms of opportunities provided by changed circumstances, rather than another problem to solve (I know, some things are just problems but I'm speaking in terms of a general rule).

Don't Panic! Things will often feel like they are about to go totally sideways. As producer or producer/director you need to be the coolest head on set. PA's won't show up. Other crew will disappear into paid work or family commitments. If possible, have back-ups or divide up a job between multiple people so that you have fallback options. We had two make-up artists who alternated nights and we had two audio recordists, each for different days. Organize this as much as possible before your shoot. Never, ever yell at people. Other than explosions or death there is a creative solution for almost anything.

Have a quiet place off set for the actors. You can't afford a trailer but it's nice to give them a place to prepare. After all everyone is going to be staring at them and all their flaws under glaring lights pretty soon. They deserve a place to chill, even if it's a bedroom with some refreshments.

Dot your i's and cross your t's. Make sure that your PM/AD has all the forms that need to be signed – and there will be lots of them: time sheets for cast, crew deal memos, cast deal memos, image release forms (so you can use images of crew captured in behind the scenes shots). You will need all these as part of your deliverables if you try to get a sales agent or distributor. If you self-distribute, it's good to cover your legal bases and have these in your files anyway. Get as many of these signed at your battle meeting prior to your first day of shooting.

INTERVIEW WITH A DOP

Daniel Stephens is a Director of Photography, as well as a Producer, Writer and Director. He has worked on many films, including El Ganzo, Helltown and The Sauce.

What is most different about shooting a microbudget from larger films?

This is a difficult question as often the two situations are different in so many big ways. Budget doesn't just have an effect on crew size and equipment available, but also day length (and thus crew morale and readiness), preparation time, locations or studio, pages per day and thus overall shoot days and on and on. Let me phrase it as a most positive and a most negative and then simply most different (neutral).

A positive by-product of a smaller budget is a smaller crew. This translates, if it's a seasoned crew (which I usually recommend), into a more nimble production and thus more efficient. It often means that more pages can be shot in a day, that the setups are (by plan and often necessity) more creative and less structured with more lights/more gear, and that we can react more quickly to serendipitous location changes (often due to weather or lighting).

A negative by-product of a smaller budget is simply less prep time. As a DP, I will prep as long as I can regardless of budget. I've often done months of research into genre lighting, camera breadth, framing, and composition for a small budget film that I've been given virtually no prep-time for. But I feel it's necessary regardless of budget, and perhaps even more-so on a shorter-shoot, to make sure that I've prepped enough to have a plan or nascent idea for every possible situation and the feeling of confidence that comes from having said plan. Inevitably something unplanned will happen and then the prep really pays off because I don't feel completely caught off-guard. Of course, when the budget is small, it's hard for other departments to prep as much as they need to or would like to. Not everyone has the time available to prep when they're not being paid for it and that can be a serious problem on a feature film.

Another negative by-product of a smaller budget is also crew size. There are times when having a larger, more experienced crew simply helps get through a difficult scene or series of scenes if there's simply a need for a lot of hands on deck. Large setups or long hauls into a location can tire out a small crew and make it less efficient very quickly. And a less efficient crew, or a tired crew isn't working at its peak and the shots/scenes will suffer.

A neutral outcome of a smaller budget, but a real difference between it and a large budget is gear. With limited funds (and at some level, they're always limited, even on a "big budget" film), problems or challenges must be solved creatively and that means that the solution isn't just sitting idly in the G&E truck. But the creative problem-solving can be a truly magnificent experience that ultimately raises the film's esthetic and bonds the camera, grip and lighting crew together. So it's not necessarily a pro or a con, it just requires a different mode of thinking.

What was your biggest challenge shooting a microbudget?

I do think it's related to prep time; to the fact that not every first in every department is going to have the prep time they want or need to do their absolute best.

I also think that the number of locations can become a problem. The script really needs to reflect what's available in the budget, and vice versa. Shooting a $750K or $1M feature film with 60 locations is going to be problematic. If there's 30 shoot days and 60 locations, that's a company move each day. That tires out a crew very quickly. Of course, this is an extreme example, but I've worked on that film and it can and does happen.

But at the $10K to $50K budget, keeping locations to a minimum is key to making a beautiful, engaging film. Too much rushing about from location to location tires out a small crew as well as the cast. It doesn't really give either group of people enough time to know a location, to really dig into it and discover its hidden secrets, to weave it fully into the story.

Location is a character; each room, doorway, hallway, picture-car, ardent field, trash-strewn street is a character and adds immeasurably to the story. These characters need time to be discovered, need time for their performances to come out. And again, on these budgets it's hard to do this in advance of shooting as there's so little prep time. So, fewer locations really lets each one become its fullest self with respect to the story and in relationship to the characters.

What did you enjoy most?

Small budgets often mean small, nimble crews. And with a small crew, everyone becomes part of a small, tight family. We eat together, we live together, we play together when there's time for that. I was working on a most delightful and yet slightly enigmatic film in San Jose del Cabo, at the very tip of the Baja Peninsula a few years ago. We were a small crew with a small budget. We all lived together in the same hotel, we rode together in the same van. We were all part of every single setup, shot and scene. We became a tight, loving family. We held each other up when we were exhausted from a magnificent day's shoot. We swam together in the Pacific Ocean and the Sea of Cortez. We nursed each other when we were sick. It was marvelous. And when you watch the film, which really only has a very few characters in it, you can feel every bit of that love and passion.

Not that this doesn't happen with a large budget, but I think the money can get in the way.

How can directors on microbudgets work more effectively with a DP to get the best possible work?

A director and DP on a microbudget film must work together as one. They're going to spend a lot of time together. Ultimately they need to have respect for each other and trust. Of course, they may have never worked together before; but if each comes to the relationship (and it is a relationship) with an open heart and open mind, then the trust and respect will come quickly. And then it's simply a question of letting each person do what they do best. The DP stays out of the director's chair and the director engages and invites the DP into all aspects of the film's visual palette. Practically, this translates into the DP being open to meeting the director in whatever way the director wishes to communicate. And from a director's perspective, it means keeping the DP informed as specifically as possible about what each scene is supposed to communicate.

The DP knows how to translate feelings and words and expressions into a visual experience, but the DP needs to have a detailed understanding of what the director envisions. Pictures work great, whether the DP and director storyboard together (which I strongly recommend) or they watch innumerable films together, noting how each film fits into their film's visual palette. They can also share photographs and paintings and literature with each other. All these things build up a collage of extant expressions that each can then refer to during discussions in prep or on set as a short-hand way of getting to a specific emotive expression that both of them feel confident the other understands.

Any other advice for DP's or filmmakers more generally thinking of making a microbudget?

Prepare. Watch every film you can that somehow relates to your film, write a synopsis of it and share it with the director. Collect images (I like to use Pinterest and also old-school binders) and arrange them by feeling, intention, literal and figurative meaning. Draw storyboards. And even better, draw them with the director sitting beside you (or on Skype with you). It doesn't matter if you can't draw. If you can't draw, then perhaps take a drawing class. It will make you a better DP. Learn to let go of gear. Gear doesn't solve problems. In fact, an over-reliance on gear often causes more problems. Find the few pieces of lighting gear that you really love, learn how to use them in every conceivable way. This will make you fast and nimble, both physically and mentally. And embrace the lightness of being that comes from a small crew, a tight script and a driven director.

ON BEGGING & SELLING

I haven't talked about post-production yet but now's the time to break the bad news: it's going to cost you as much or more as your production phase. But there's good news: your production phase is a great time to beg your friends for money to complete your film.

Many people use crowdfunding to raise money for their production before they go to camera. If you're not Zach Braff, crowdfunding for a name brand show, I would strongly suggest that you don't try to crowdfund before you go to camera – unless you have a strong niche film, like a social-commentary documentary. Here's why: nobody cares. That's not quite right. Your friends and family care. But that's pretty much it. Think about it – when a bunch of friends form a new band and play their first gig, who shows up? Their friends and family. Nobody shows up off their posters. Why would they? It's the same with your crowdfunding effort.

What's more, your friends and family will be more inspired to support you when you've actually done something, as opposed to "I have this idea for a film I'd like to make." Instead you're telling them – "hey, we're shooting this movie and we've funded the production ourselves but we need help with the post-production." Like it or not, people help people who help themselves. That's not to say you can't raise money from friends and family before you go to camera, just that it needs a different approach, as I outlined above.

But the most important reason to run your crowdfunding campaign *during* your production is that you are producing tons of legitimate material every single day to promote your crowdfunding effort. If you haven't run a crowdfunding campaign before it can be summarized like this: you put up a nice intro video and a bunch of text that almost nobody will read. Then you bug the shit out of your friends for 30 days (and a crowdfunding campaign shouldn't be longer than that, for your own sanity as much as for maintaining momentum).

The great thing about crowdfunding during production is that you're not just saying the same things over and over and over to your friends and family. You're sharing with them an exciting experience that comes with photos, videos, outtakes, a production diary (did I mention you should write a production diary while your shooting, every day if possible?). So you're not just sending them a thousand emails that say "please give me money" – though you should definitely personally email every single person whom you've ever met and solicit money from them during your crowdfunding campaign. You should do it even if that means writing the emails beforehand and scheduling them in your email program to send after the campaign starts.

And every one of those emails ought to contain a personal note to the person – how's your dog? How's your ingrown toenail? Did you ever get the backyard nuclear reactor to work? After your personal note, then you can have the more canned, boilerplate money-begging form letter. I sent both emails and Facebook messages to *hundreds* of people; people I hadn't seen from high school, people who were loosely related to my wife's cousin through a marriage that ended. I was shameless. And often I was surprised who gave cash and how much. If people don't want to give you money they'll ignore your email and forget about it. You're just giving them the opportunity to be awesome, what they do is up to them.

So, doing this how much can you raise? $30,000? $50,000? $75K? Try maybe $5,000. Seriously. Don't lie to yourself. And don't ask for an amount based on what you need to do x, y, and z. That's what we did on our first campaign and we had to stretch the truth and pretend that we met our target when it was obvious to anyone who looked that we missed it by 35%. It didn't help that we started our crowdfunding campaign almost a year after we wrapped production. Don't be like us. It's embarrassing and depressing.

Think about what you can realistically raise from everyone you know – then divide it by half. We asked for $12,000 with our first campaign and raised just over $7,000. On our second campaign we said that we wanted to raise $5,000 because we thought we could probably repeat what we had done with the first movie. We raised almost $10,000. See what happened there? It was an achievable goal and we surpassed it. We raised excitement with all our material during production. And people got excited as we closed in rapidly on our goal and then wanted to be part of pushing us over the top. And we felt great because we met our target. We wrapped our fundraising campaign a day or two after the big wrap party, which was part of the fundraising (free booze and food for cast and crew plus guests, $20 all you can drink draft for everyone else). What a fabulous way to end a shoot – a blow-out party, a successful shoot that got everything in the can, and soundly meeting and surpassing our fundraising goal.

So, what crowdfunding platform should you use? Doesn't matter. All that matters is which one charges the lowest commissions, though they're probably all the same. Unless you find a way to get your commissions down below all the main platforms, I would go with a known name like IndieGoGo or Kickstarter. I think people still believe that just by putting up their project on IndieGoGo that a bunch of people will find them and fund their campaign. Unless you're selling some newfangled technical gadget that makes your bed in the morning or allows you to clone your dead dog, it's not going to happen. It's all down to you.

One final note on crowfunding and maintaining your sanity. When you come up with your "incentives" – the different rewards people get for donating various amounts of money – do yourself a favor and keep it simple. Don't come up with things that require all kinds of work – designing and printing t-shirts or creating special products, like "limited edition DVD signed by the cast and crew". It seems like a really cool idea, until you have to fulfill it and then it's a nightmare.

Keep it focused on things related directly to the movie and that don't require you sitting around licking stamps, etc. The reality on a microbudget is that almost all of the people who will support you are connected to you somehow (have I said this enough times?). They are giving you money because they want YOU and YOUR PROJECT to succeed. Not because they want a tchotchke. Digital downloads of the film are good. Free tickets to the premiere. An associate producer credit for a $500 contribution. That kind of thing.

7 IT AIN'T OVER YET, BABY

Wow, that shoot was exhilarating wasn't it? You shot everything you needed to and you have a film. Uh, no. You still have the even longer process of post-production to go through now. And that can take you more time and money than your production. There's four ways you can handle post-production:

Do it yourself.
Get volunteers
Go to a post house
Hire freelancers

Probably you're going to do a mix of several of these. I helped cut the assembly on both of our films. But I didn't want to edit because film's strength is that it is a collective effort. Just like it's important for you to get an outside set of eyes to look over your script, it's important to have someone impartial who has distance from your material as an editor. They will see things that you won't and bring great suggestions to the table. They aren't just there to implement what you say, they are a collaborator on your final film. Remember: a film is made three times – when it's written, when it's shot and when it's edited.

For our first film we paid an amazing editor to take us from assembly to final cut. On our second film we used an amazing editor who works professionally as an assistant editor but wanted the experience and donated her services during her spare time. We also used a post-house for the color correct and audio on our first film. On our second we hired freelancers. Post on our first film cost us way more but it came with certain benefits.

Paying an editor meant that he was dedicated to us, more or less. We could sit down with him for days on end and go through each scene and tweak. On our second film we had moved out of the country so we had to do our editing remotely. Because of the time difference and because our editor had a full-time job at a post house, it meant it took way longer. She would send us cuts and then we would have to find the time – more difficult when it's not a series of scheduled meetings that you make time for – and sit down with the film making notes.

We used Wipster, which at the time cost about $15/month (until they jacked the price to unjustifiable levels), and allows you to make notes right on the video in the timeline, rather than writing down timecodes and notes in a word processor. It was super helpful and worth the money. But it's not the same as being able to be in the room. The second strategy we used was to work with her through Skype. She would output short segments and upload them to dropbox. We would watch them and give her notes on the spot. It meant that while one segment was outputting or uploading, we were actively working on another segment. This was a much more rapid way of working and allowed us to test out more things. Wipster was good for crafting the story but Skype editing this way is way better for polishing.

When it came to color correcting, audio mixing, etc. we had always heard that you can go to post houses and they love to help out little films. That's true and not true. If you've made the next *Blair Witch Project* or perhaps *Tangerine*, a film shot on an iPhone 5S, they want to get in on the action and have their name associated with your project. They might do it for an executive producer credit and a share of the profits. If, like us, you've made a decent film that probably won't make any money....well, not so much. The post house we went with *did* give us a great deal, probably half or less of what we would have paid at full price. And the quality was great but it still cost us an arm and a leg, more than we had raised in our IndieGoGo campaign.

With our second film we went to Upwork.com, a freelance hiring hall where you can post a job and then solicit proposals from people. You can get people from all over the world, in places where their overhead is low and so their prices are much lower. This is how we found our colorist and audio mixer in Spain, where we had moved. The benefit is that you can find very good people for very cheap rates. The drawback is that they are probably somewhere in the world where you can't be present and you have to coordinate notes remotely. We ended up paying a quarter of what we paid with the first film but we aren't able to sit in high-end suites with big, color correct screens and great sound (not to mention free canapes and a wet bar!).

As with everything it's a balance. I would personally suggest getting an editor through your own devices then going to a post house to see what they can do for you. If they can't cut you a deal that fits within your budget – and doesn't give away the store in terms of rights – then I would explore local and international freelancers through something like Upwork. Actually, let's be honest: on our next film, I'll start with Upwork.

LET'S TALK MUSIC

Unless you're shooting DOGME style, you're going to want music in your film to some extent, even if it's only music playing on stereos or headphones in the film. That means dealing with two types of music is probably on the cards: composed music and pre-existing tracks. Just like with other elements of post you can find people on Upwork if you can't find people locally through your connections. Before you hire anyone make sure to listen to their portfolio. You want to see their range and their abilities. And talk to them, you want to make sure that your vision and your personalities jive. You want them to bring their own unique vision to the project but you don't want to be fighting with them the whole time. Know beforehand exactly how much money you can spend and be upfront about it. We paid our composer $1500 with more money promised if we made any net profits.

My big point however is about pre-existing music. And I have only one point to make about it: don't pay for music. We got a very competent and professional music supervisor for *A Brand New You*. He made a bunch of useful suggestions and found us a lot of the music that we used in the movie. And he insisted that we pay the musicians. Not an unreasonable demand per se. But it added 30% to our budget (ie. several thousand dollars), for music that we could have gotten for free by and large. It's not that I don't think that musicians should be paid for their music, because I do. But you don't have the money and there are ba-zillions of great musicians out there who just want their music to reach an audience. Sure, if you make a soundtrack afterwards and sell it on iTunes you should give them the money. But are you really going to do that? And the chances of your film making more than just its money back is pretty slim (actually, the chances of your film making its money back at all is slim). You're not ripping them off because you're not profiting off them because you're not profiting (at least it's very unlikely and that's not the point).

I would suggest instead that you put the word out – on social media, on Craigslist, amongst your friends. Contact your favorite local band. Look for music on Band Camp. If you put out an ad, ask for the kind of music that you're looking for and make clear that you won't be able to pay. You will get a lot of great music, much more than you can use. This is not a license to rip people off. If, in the end, you can help out these musicians who are helping you out – with money, promotion, etc. – then you most certainly should.

One more thing: make sure you get signed contracts. There are two forms you need to sign for every song that you use: a master use license and a sync license. Make sure you get both of these signed (even if you are the musician) or, again, you will never be able to sell your film. This goes into your deliverables kit for a distributor or even if you self-distribute, to protect yourself. A composer's contract should have rights attribution as part of the contract.

LAST THING, REALLY

You had a photographer on set taking stills as well as behind the scenes. Now, as you approach final cut, you will use some of those stills to get key art made. Getting a poster design can cost you up to $1200. Or you can use a service like designcrowd.com to get a poster design. You post your "brief" – a blurb about the movie, its genre and tone, provide some film posters that you'd like it modeled on stylistically – along with some images and then designers will post their ideas. You can ask them to make some changes and trim it down to the top five, then ask your community to vote on your favorite (another marketing opportunity!). Just be careful with the voting because maybe you've got a bunch of friends with really bad taste. We saved our own votes till the end and then made sure to push the one over the top that we really liked.

The important thing is that for $350 we got a really great poster and the designer was even very gracious to make some changes months afterwards. When you start submitting to festivals, they will want both stills from on-set as well as key art (ie. posters). The size that we had to send out was 24Wx36H inches. If you don't have Photoshop to alter the images afterwards, ask the designer to give you a full size, a web-sized and a thumbnail sized version (that last two you'll want as useable files in the form of .png or .jpg) If you get into festivals – and you don't have editing software – you'll want to go back to your designer and ask them to put your beautiful laurels on the poster (festivals send you graphics files with the laurels for just this purpose).

8 SPREAD THE LOVE

Yay, you're done! You have a completed film. First things first: relish the moment. You have done what very few people have, even in this age of cheap, accessible gear and social media. You really need to pat yourself on the back and celebrate how awesome you are.

Ok, are you done? Now it's time to think about what to do with your lovely. The traditional avenue is to send it out to festivals and build it up some buzz and pedigree. So, the first thing you do is send it out to SXSW and Sundance and Cannes and Toronto and maybe Teluride because they deserve to see your film too.

Not so fast.

TEARS FOR TIERS

I'm sure your film is wonderful and unique and powerful. But there's something we need to talk about: festivals are political, commercial machines integrated into the Hollywood behemoth. PLUS there's a lot of films out there. Thousands submit to first tier festivals for barely a hundred feature slots. And, what's more, most of the slots, certainly all the prime time ones, are filled by studio and "independent" films made for millions of dollars with A-list stars. You're up against some heavy hitters.

Festival programming, at the big festivals in particular, is heavily political. If they want the latest film that will draw audiences and be loved by critics, well then they have to take the lesser films by the same studio or production company. And they want to draw audiences. The easy way is to get the newest film by some big star, even though it might be a stinker. I don't want to suggest that first tier festivals only take big budget, crappy movies, they don't. But it is very hard to get into them without someone pulling for you who is on the inside. There are very few slots for outsider films, especially those with microbudgets. Usually a handful get in that have been championed by a programmer or festival director and/or that are seen as truly outstanding in one way or another. *George Washington* by David Gordon Green (*Pineapple Express*, *Joe*) was rejected by Sundance. So were *Swingers* and *Paranormal Activity*. So, if you get rejected, you're in good company.

That's OK though. Remember, you made this movie because you were on the outside of the Hollywood system. The big festivals are part of the Hollywood system. That's not to say that you shouldn't apply to a few of them – you could be the one that gets in to Sundance and then I'd look like a shmuck if I'd discouraged you from submitting. But, seriously, don't bet the emotional farm on getting into a first tier festival with your little film. And don't blow your whole festival budget submitting to the top 10 festivals in the world.

Luckily, there are literally thousands of festivals out there – second tier, third tier, regional, genre, and more. They also get hundreds of entries, so getting in is certainly not automatic. But at least you're not competing against Brad Pitt or Robert Downey Jr. or Helen Mirren.

Do your research. MovieMaker Magazine puts out a "50 festivals worth the entry fee" list every year. Check out other films in your budget range and genre and see which festivals they got into. Make a list in a spreadsheet to keep track of submission deadlines, fees, location, etc. The two big submission websites are Withoutabox.com and Filmfreeway.com. WAB has the worst interface ever and they squeeze filmmakers hard but they do have some festivals that Filmfreeway doesn't have. Filmfreeway has a much more filmmaker friendly attitude, lots of festivals and a really user-friendly interface. There is also Film Festival Life, which has a lot of international film festivals. How to approach submitting, once you've tried the big fests?

Blitz the smaller festivals. By that I mean, submit to like a 100 of them. Sounds crazy right? You were thinking you'd submit to one or two dozen and get into 8 or 10 and you'd be golden. Well, maybe you will. And maybe you won't. You want to build "pedigree" for your film by getting some legit laurels to put on your poster, not to mention have the festival experience. Don't set some arbitrarily low number and then feel depressed when you don't get into any of them. Remember, there are *thousands* of feature films out there submitting to festivals every year. Maybe you've made something so spectacular that nobody can say no. Or maybe you've made a good film, at about the same level as a whole bunch of other good films. Then it's going to come down to the taste of the programmers, along with other considerations (returning filmmakers, hometown filmmakers, films with a name cast member in them, etc).

It will cost you a bit of cash – we spent about $1200 on festival submissions. Some festivals are $100 (we avoided these) but there are also some great festivals below $50 and international festivals in many places outside of North America are free. We submitted for free to Comedy Cluj in Romania and were accepted. It was an awesome festival with incredible guest services and unbelievably top-notch volunteers. They had free food and booze, day trips for filmmakers and lots of opportunities for networking. If your state or country has a film body that promotes and/or supports local films in other ways, check and see if they have relationships with some festivals. Telefilm in Canada, for instance has relationships that allow Canadian filmmakers to submit for free to a number of prestigious film festivals, including Cannes.

SHINING & SMILING

There's two parts to submitting to festivals. There's the fact that you want to get laurels to put on your poster because it gives you a shine. Besides the big festivals, almost nobody outside of the biz knows one from the next. Even most people in the biz don't know a solid regional with a great track record from a festival put on by some high school horror fans. Getting into festivals builds excitement for your main audience – the people at home who liked your Facebook page and contributed to your IndieGoGo campaign.

The other part is attending festivals. If you get into festivals you should certainly attend at least some of them. We went to about half, I think. It costs you some money and very few provide you with flight or accommodation. But even if there's no perks, the experience is amazing and will be great for your self-esteem as a filmmaker. It is also an opportunity to do what you're really there to do – connect with an international filmmaking community.

Festivals are great places to network. Sure you might meet distributors or sales agents (don't count on it, they're more likely to contact you afterwards if at all). But mostly you will meet other filmmakers, perhaps festival programmers, actors, etc. And, of course, people who will love your film, which is a buzz. You are there to build community and potential collaborators. I went to two festivals in Texas, the first time was a bit of a letdown, except that I met an awesome filmmaker from Texas and we kept in touch. She helped me to get into the Victoria Texas Indie Film Fest, an ostensibly smaller festival and it was awesome. I met some great people passionate about film and ended up on the jury the following year. I story-edited a film by the founder of the festival. It was a real high point for me. They are an excellent festival with a real community of filmmakers around, a great handcrafted award and lots of parties and networking with other filmmakers. Definitely worth submitting to VTXIFF.

When you go to festivals, there's a couple things you should know:

Don't hire publicists. People say you should do this and I think it's a total waste of cash. Ask the festival programmer who contacted you if there's some local press who cover the festival and get their contact info. Send them a press kit. Unless maybe you're at Sundance what are you hoping to achieve with a publicist that you couldn't do yourself? Print up some flyers advertising your movie – like send them to vista print online and get a couple of hundred made – and hand them out to people at parties. Mingle. Party. Promote your film. Network and meet people. A publicist will run you $5K or more and unless you've got buzz already, probably won't help much. You'd be better off hiring street teams to leaflet people about your movie.

Don't expect to fill an enormous theater with thousands of people wanting to see your movie. Expect to be in a half to quarter full, small theater (at best) with some enthusiastic people. The Q&A we did in Romania, for about 50 people, was awesome and inspiring. Remember, you aren't Stephen Spielberg and you don't have Brad Pitt in your movie – why would someone in some other country, who has never heard of you, go to see it if there's no buzz around it. Be super-grateful for the people who did, in spite of your lack of star power. They took a chance on your little film.

Lastly, watch out for scam festivals. There's a lot of these and, unfortunately, the festival submission platforms like filmfreeway do not really vet for which are authentic, if small, and which are two guys counting your money before screening your film in their livingroom. The platforms don't care; they get their cut either way. Use some due diligence – I say this from experience.

INTERVIEW WITH A FESTIVAL PROGRAMMER
Anthony Pedone is the founder and head programmer of the Victoria Texas Independent Film Festival. He also founded The Film Exchange to provide resources and gear for filmmakers who want to shoot in the Victoria area. He produced *The Strongest Man*, **which went to Sundance and directed the recently completed microbudget feature,** *An American In Texas*.

What are some of the best things you've seen in microbudget films as a programmer?

The unbridled need by humans to immerse themselves in collaborative endeavors, and that the need for creativity in people's lives is undeniable. I have seen people relive trauma in their lives, by recreating horrible experiences in films, and watch a video of their healing as they come to terms with their trauma through the filmmaking process. Mostly I take great pleasure in watching people realize their dreams of making a film. I remind myself that all of these films are completed, and there must be MANY more that are not. Any of these microbudget filmmakers, I would draft them into my army when the end of the world comes, because they are going to be the survivors, because they are blinded by passion, and hell bent on problem solving.

What catches your eye when you're watching microbudgets?

I think a strong opening is key for programmers to watch your film. You have to grab them right away, and I don't necessarily mean a smash up, car crash, exploding head type of thing (although that will get you noticed for sure if it is done well). Find the interesting things and feature them. If you are shooting in the desert, I want to see the vastness of this place. I notice when filmmakers have patience and smother the view.

Lots of microbudget's make the mistake of creating claustrophobia. Establish the world we are about to be in. Great opening music, and visuals are a must. Don't put fancy fonts for your title sequence, but a great opening or title credits, or musical choice will definitely benefit your films chances. All of that aside though, strong acting, and story are the things that get you to the end of the film. If the actors are strong, and they are invested in the project you will hold most programmers attention until the final act.

What do you think are the most common mistakes that microbudget filmmakers make?

Cutting corners with sound, camera and technical aspects seems to be the big mistakes that I have made, and learned that those things must be there, or you are fighting your back from the beginning. It isn't fair to your story, your actors or the viewer to take that kind of liberty. If you don't have those things, don't shoot it yet.

What would be your one piece of advice for microbudget filmmakers in relation to submitting to festivals?

Pay the damn submission fee if you are submitting a feature. We are not, and cannot be bothered with your story of the "filmmaking struggle". I am a filmmaker, and I know the struggle. I have made films too, and I pay submission fees to festivals that I want to be in. You are very short sighted to believe that you have done something amazing because you made your film for cheap, and now as the programmer, the guy going to potentially show your film in a theatre, is the guy you crossed off your budget when "saving money".

When you are reaching out to a programmer, remember that the stress you were under when filming is probably at a similar level for that fest director/programmer right now, as hundreds of people are hitting his inbox with requests for free shit, when he or she is trying to plan an event that is going to cost him thousands of dollars and hundreds of his own hours for very little pay.

All of these inbox stories are very similar. Don't put yourself in that category right away, unless you have a personal connection with that programmer or director. Personalize before you ask for a handout. I mean meet this programmer in person first. Go to their fest, meet them at a first tier festival, or have a producing partner that has that connection. All that aside, if you cannot afford the fee, ask for a discount. I always grant discounts, but seldom do I grant waivers unless I know the filmmaker, or they have programmed here before. It is a two way street and us lower tier fests are on the same street with you filmmakers.

If you don't know someone at SXSW, Sundance, Tribeca…. get to know someone there. Go to film week at IFP, go to Sundance, SXSW or any of the top tier fests, and get to know the landscape. It is a part of the process, and if you are not the networking type, you need one of those guys/gals. You NEED that. One last time, you cannot and should not do this all by yourself. Find a producing partner, and preferably one that has made a few of these small films, or is a good people person, and can break through the walls that are up around everyone in this industry.

Any other words of advice for filmmakers looking to make their first feature?

Have you made a short? If you haven't, then do so, with your feature film idea. You don't have to show it to anyone, or at festivals, but make it. Make a trailer. It is easier to get people to get in a car that may or may not be headed off the cliff if you can demonstrate to your passengers that you can indeed drive, first.

9 BRING IT HOME, SEND IT AWAY

Once you've spent maybe a year on the festival circuit you're going to want to bring your film home and beyond. I have limited experience with distribution but I want to share with you what I do know from our first film. Hopefully this will help you avoid the pitfalls out there.

You probably have some debts left from making your movie and traveling to exotic and wonderful places with it. Not to mention the costs of making it. And, funny enough, the last place you will show it before "going wide" will be your hometown. But now it's back, what do you do?

Organize a screening in an appropriate sized venue. It's always better to sell-out than have a half empty theater. Book a space that can fit less than what you believe you can sell. We packed out a theatre for 180 people for our first film and had to tell people that we were sold out. We had considered contacting film schools and offering free tickets to the show but we had to scrap that because there wasn't room. Just as with crowdfunding, aim lower and surpass your goals. If you book a 100 seat theatre and sell-out you will feel much better than if you book a 300 seat theatre and only sell 135 tickets.

You shouldn't try to play a hometown festival unless it's got some serious cache, like TIFF or SXSW or even a major second tier festival. A smaller festival isn't going to get you a distributor and they get the money from the door while you bring all the people (and paid the entry fee). Instead, organize your own hometown premiere. Sell tickets using an online ticket service (this is way better than getting people to click "attend" on a Facebook event page, though you should create one of these too and link it to your online ticket service using the Facebook "action" button). Remember to contact your IndieGoGo contributors for their free tickets – and if they say no or don't get back to you, then sell their tickets. Make it a big deal. Rent a red carpet. Buy big posters and a step/repeat (which is like a pull-down blind/poster that you can pose in front of for photos). Dress up. Have a photographer taking photos at the event. Have an after party.

This is also a good time to get some reviews of your movie. Send out press releases and try to get local papers and web press to write reviews and interviews prior to the screening. Especially if you've got laurels it's possible to get some decent coverage/reviews for your hometown screening. You should also be pro-active about finding reviews. Look up other films in your genre, niche and budget range and see who reviewed their film. There's a wonderful Toronto filmmaker named Ingrid Veninger who has a number of films. She's known as the "Queen of DIY Filmmaking" (she might have made up that label herself, I don't know. If she did it was a brilliant piece of branding because it stuck). We went to her website and checked out the names and websites of people who reviewed her film. We did the same with a number of other films in the DIY/no-budget realm. Then we looked them up – or the websites that they wrote for – and sent them a personal email asking them if they would review our award-winning feature film. We got several reviews this way and then we grabbed pull-quotes from the reviews to put on our website. "Audacious and groundbreaking" that kind of thing (I just made that up, nobody said that about our movie).

This could be your only post-festival screening so do it all up and get as much as you can out of it.

WILL IT LIVE ON?

You may or may not get distribution beyond what you do yourself. There's a good chance you won't unless you organize it yourself in non-traditional venues and self-distribution platforms. There was a time several years ago where crappy, microbudget horror films would get a sales agent and then get sold in the international marketplace. Those days are over and now the quality and SFX have to be top notch to make a sale. Not to say that you can't do that for little money but making a genre film for pennies doesn't get you as far as it once did. But let me tell you a few things about getting distribution based on our experience.

If you get into a few festivals and win an award or two you may well be contacted by companies offering distribution. Avoid companies that "offer" you services that you have to pay for. If you're giving them money their incentive is to get money out of you, not sell your picture.

If you are contacted by a sales agent that's great. But know that you will have to spend probably several thousand dollars getting together all the deliverables that they need – notarized contracts, music & effects tracks (ie. tracks that have all the sounds except for the dialogue so that it can be dubbed in a foreign language, which costs a bucket load of cash because someone has to foley your entire film), Errors & Omissions insurance (to make sure distributors can't be sued if you accidentally filmed a can of Pepsi in that scene with the naked bank heist, which they think will make them look bad), title searches, quality control reports (which you may have to have done more than once because they found some stupid small shit on the first pass that nobody would have noticed while watching your film on Netflix as they were trying to get laid with whomever they invited over to chill with them). You have to pay for all this and while, in the end, it *might* get you a sale, it might not. If it does it probably won't be for very much. You have to ask yourself: would those thousands of dollars have been more useful marketing my film through a self-distribution platform (or paying a company like Distribber to get your film on iTunes, etc) that actually got my film out? I hope our sales agent proves me wrong. I will say this one thing for getting a sales agent – you can tell people at festivals when you're trying to get them to fund your next picture: "yeah, we have a sales agent for *Monster In Size Nine Shoes* and they're looking at some offers right now." Cache does have some value.

You can self-distribute through one of the many platforms that exist. But you will be doing all the publicity and marketing. Actually, if you get on iTunes you'll still be doing a lot of marketing to get people to watch it. Platforms like iTunes bring credibility, provide some visibility on their storefront and people feel safe buying stuff from them. Before we got our sales agent we used Gumroad because they charged the lowest commissions ($10/month and 3.5% commission) and allowed us to rent or sell as well as offering functionality like offering discounts. There's also VHX, Distrify and others. We made about $1000 by renting our video through Gumroad. If we'd spent the thousands of dollars that we've spent on providing deliverables to a sales agent doing some more Facebook marketing, who knows. Live and learn.

If you want to do theatrical screenings there are services, the most pre-eminent being TUGG. If you go this route you will have to get a Digital Cinema Package (DCP) created during or after post-production, which could cost you about $1000 – that was what we paid to the post-house. But, frankly, unless you've got a built-in niche audience, as with a social issues documentary this seems like a waste of time. Do you have an audience in Chicago or Austin or Vancouver that is big enough to demand your film be played in a local 150-seat cinema? If you do then TUGG will, based on voting, organize all the logistics for you – for a fee of course. But if you have an audience big enough for a theatrical screening in just one or two places then you can probably organize the logistics yourself. If you have more than that, then TUGG can be useful.

There are some cool ideas and experiments out there with touring films, sometimes in conjunction with other acts, like bands. Digital projectors mean that you can get quality screenings in non-traditional venues like bars or community centers, parks or a back alley. I'd love to see more of this and see a real network of microbudget screenings. I think there's an audience for it. But I'm not in a position to innovate this model or travel around in a VW bus projecting movies onto the walls of buildings. But maybe you are, in which case do it. It could be an incredible experience and really facilitate a film movement that is sorely needed as a counterweight to Hollywood formula films.

MORE ON MARKETING

If you don't get a distribution deal or a sales agent, you will likely be thinking about what next to do after your hometown premiere. This is a tough call. I totally get it. You want your film to go as far and wide as possible. It was a lot of hard work and you made it because you had something important to say (even if it's a light-hearted comedy). At the very least you want to have the maximum impact with your little film. You're going to have to sit down with your team and/or your investors – if they're not one and the same – and decide what makes the most sense. There is no shame in saying: "We went to x number of festivals and we had a great premiere. We got some decent reviews online etc. This is as far as we can go with this film. Let's put it up on YouTube and give it away." If you decide to self-distribute you will be dedicating probably thousands of dollars and hundreds of hours of time to marketing it. That money and time may go nowhere when it could be used towards making your next film. As the wise Kenny Rogers used to say "you gotta know when to hold 'em, know when to fold 'em."

If you do decide to go forward with self-distribution, you can utilize some of the platforms I've noted above. Both Gumroad and VHX are easy to use and Gumroad has a lot of functionality for lead generation (email lists) and merchandise, if you're so bold. You can also approach Distribber, which is an aggregator that will try to get your movie up on a bunch of different platforms – iTunes, Netflix, Hulu, Google Play, et al. They will charge you a one-time fee and if none of the platforms acquire your film they will refund the fee, minus $120 for processing. However, whether you get your film on an established platform OR decide to go the route of self-distribution, you will still have to drive traffic to your film with marketing. iTunes, etc. will not market your film for you, other than perhaps putting it on their front page. So, how do you drive traffic.

OK, this is a mouthful of stuff. I suggest being well-rested and clear-headed before you start this. Maybe make a strong coffee and go somewhere quiet.

I've mentioned above Facebook and Google Ads. I've never taken a course in Google Ads and tried to use it once and found it extremely complex. You can easily spend your money and not generate any traffic. If you know someone who knows Google Ads, you might consider it.

You can also hire social media/online marketers through Upwork who know this stuff. I would just make sure that you hire someone who has lots of good reviews and a high star rating. We made the mistake of going with someone cheap and it was a fiasco – they posted a bunch of unrelated content to our Facebook page, messed around with our permissions and then demanded hundreds of dollars. We refused and they backed down. Then we had to change all the passwords on all of our social media. Our money was refunded but it was disheartening and time-consuming. It's worth paying more for someone who knows what they're doing and does it well.

Facebook is a much easier platform to use that has a set-up wizard for a business page and ads account. You just go to https://business.facebook.com and start the process – you should have done this, as I argued above, before your film even went to camera. Once you have a Facebook "fan page", you will have to create an Ads Account with payment info, etc. Again, very easy to do, especially if you have a Paypal account (which are also easy to set-up). Now you need to start targeting your audience.

You will want to create an audience – so you go to the "Audiences" link in the upper left hand pull down menu. On the Audience page you will create a "saved audience". Once you are here you're going to determine the demographics of the audience you're targeting. You can choose age, gender, location and interest groups. If you have a niche film directed at, say, Christians, you can search for all the relevant demographic groups on Facebook that accord with your niche. For instance there's a Christian film industry interest group that has 1.6 million people within it. Maybe there are specific magazines or online blogs that cater to people who watch Christian films or who are fans of Christian movie stars.

You don't want to go too wide – I'd say less than 2 million people. Facebook will keep a running tally along the side of the Audience window as you work. Facebook is going to place your ad in front of this interest group, based on your daily budget, and then its algorithms will try to figure out who amongst these are the best targets, using other data points (maybe its Christians in Wyoming or Christians who love tennis, etc). If you go too wide and you're only spending $10-$20/day, it is much harder for Facebook to narrow down the best sub-groups amongst the 10 million people you're targeting – because your ad will only reach 1,000-3,000 people per day.

You might also consider experimenting with targeting – if your Christian or LGBTQ or African-American, etc. film is located somewhere in particular or has an obvious sub-group (like tennis or firefighters, etc.) you might try your ad out with two different targets to see which performs better. In general you're going to want to experiment and I'll go into this more below.

TWO STRATEGIES

Once you have created your Facebook Page and set up some Saved Audiences, you will have to decide on your marketing strategy. You can either market your film directly to your audience or you can use a funnel model. Marketing directly is pretty straightforward. Test out different ads with different text and different images/videos and see which perform the best. Maybe in one you will use a still photo from your film. In another you will put your movie trailer. Run them for a week or so with the same budget and targeting the same demographic and see which does better.

There's an easy way to do this. Create an ad campaign and put in your Saved Audience and then all the details, images, text, daily budget and click accept. Your ad campaign will be created. Now you can click on the campaign and inside that campaign will be an "Ad Set" and if you click on that Ad Set you will be at the actual ad. You wan't to duplicate the Ad Set. You will see on the right hand side of the box with the Ad Set name that a little pencil appears. It will invite you to "edit ad set" or "create similar ad set." Create a similar ad set and then edit it, changing the details that you want different – a video instead of a production still, etc. Similarly, you can create one ad set, using your saved audience and another with a different saved audience to test the best performing demographic. Only test one difference at a time so you can measure – don't change your ad content AND your audience or you won't know if it's the audience that worked better or your ad copy.

This is easier if your film has an obvious niche. If your film doesn't have an obvious niche you might target people who love the genre of your film – horror or romance or ghost story or mumblecore, etc. (mumblecore is a pretty small audience – less than 7,000 – I checked). Brainstorm with your marketer or your team to think about who makes the most sense to target.

Another strategy is to create a funnel model of marketing. A funnel is probably how you found out about Microbudget Film Lab. We created a blog post that was free and would interest our niche, no budget filmmakers like us. Then we re-marketed the free ebook to people who went to our blog post and read it. Then, when people downloaded the ebook we got their email addresses and marketed them the *Complete Training & Production Kit* both through email and by targeting them on Facebook through ads. There's two parts to this strategy - technical and creative. Let's talk creative first and then how to implement it.

So, you've made a film about LGBTQ firefighters and because of this you're aware of the issues they face, in an often very male workplace that isn't always open to LGBTQ people (that's an assumption on my part, I have no idea). Maybe you've even tried marketing the film directly to this demographic and not had much luck. So, you're going to warm up your audience with a blog that will talk about the issues they face, the struggles in the workplace, in the union, in the community, etc. You create a blog post about, say, "5 Ways To Survive Being An LGBTQ Firefighter". Something that offers an awareness of the issues and some solutions to this group – real solutions, don't just make stuff up. It doesn't have to be a social issue, it could be "the best Christian tennis films ever made". Relevant and useful. You're trying to offer something valuable that will help people – and not only to help them but also to develop a relationship with them. And don't make the blog post too long – no more than 1500 words. You want people to read to the end.

As a side note: You can track things like the amount of time spent on your page – to see if most people are reading to the end (assuming about 200 words per minute) by creating a Google Analytics account, setting up a tracking pixel with Google and then getting the code that it automatically generates and putting it in the global header of your blog. There are lots of articles on this for different platforms, like Wordpress, that will walk you through the process and Google will walk you through getting a tracking pixel. Now Google will track all your traffic, how long people stay on each page, etc. You just go to Google Analytics, go down to Behavior > Site Content > All Pages. It will show you each page that has been visited and how long people on average stayed on the page. If you have a 1000 word article, they will need approx. 5 minutes to read it. Doesn't have to be everyone reading through to the end but at least more than half the people visiting your page, ie. say about 3 minutes average. Keep tweaking your blog post, editing it, etc. until you get a good read through rate. If you're not a great writer stylistically, write up what you want to say and hire a copywriter through Upwork for very little money to make your blog post shine. Again, remember it's better to hire someone who is well-rated and pay a little more for good quality work.

At the bottom of the blog post you put a link to a guidebook on being an LGBTQ firefighter, resources for work related stress, etc. To get the free, very useful guidebook, they give you their email address in return – it doesn't *have* to be a guidebook, that's just one suggestion; it can be many things, use your imagination. What would your target audience consider useful/appealing information to have? You can do this through Gumroad as well, which allows you to sell merch as well as renting your movie. Just set the price at zero and they charge you no commissions. You can also try to go directly to selling your film at the bottom of your blog posts. But if you go the step of getting "leads" (ie. emails) you can now develop an email marketing campaign, either by sending out direct, personal style emails to people or by creating a newsletter. You can set this up on Mail Chimp – it's very straightforward. You have to be careful not to spam people and they have to be able to unsubscribe, otherwise Mail Chimp will cut off your account. That's just the law on spamming. If your first offer, called in an "opt-in bribe", doesn't work, just keep trying. Tweak your pitch. Offer something different. If they don't click through to it on your website, you can re-market to them through Facebook (explained below).

So, now you have their email address. Maybe in your next step you offer them something else – some other resources, an interview with an LGBTQ firefighter with whom you spoke in the research for your movie. Be creative and make it interesting. And make a note in your email that you've created this award-winning film about the issue and it's almost ready for release; build up anticipation. You can do this more than once, offering multiple "bonuses" to keep them interested and deepen your relationship with your potential audience.

OK, so you've got several dozen email addresses and getting a few more every day. Now you can start marketing your film through email. You can set up timed release of emails through Mail Chimp, so that when they "opt-in" they get the link right away for the ebook or interview or whatever. Then two days later they get the bonus content. Then three days after that they get the notice of the film being ready for download. Offer them a special time-limited deal – 7 days or two weeks at half the price (you can set up deal codes through Gumroad to give people special discounts). You can also set it up so that once they click through they no longer get further marketing emails to rent or buy the film and get sent from the lead list into a customer list (once they're customers who have seen your movie, you can change your marketing to them – Would they like to host a local screening? Would they like to buy merchandise like t-shirts? Contests? Updates on what's happening with this film or perhaps the next one? As you can see there is a lot of moving parts to this marketing machine but you can do it and if not, it's still useful for you to know the basic process so that you can communicate with the online marketer whom you hire through Upwork, etc.

LET'S GET TECHNICAL

That's the creative (and some technical) elements to your funnel marketing strategy. Let's talk tech. So, your first ad on Facebook goes out to everyone in your target demographic. Now you start to get people reading your blog, one dozen, two dozen, a hundred. You want to market the opt-in bribe (or your film if you want to go directly to this) to them and only them. This is the funnel – you're going wide and narrowing it down to maximize your marketing impact – and save money.

To track who has been where and when you will need to create a Facebook Tracking Pixel. When you do this for your blog post it will then generate some code that, like the Google Pixel, will go in your global header. Gumroad offers tutorials on this and it's pretty straightforward. Now Facebook will know everyone who visits any page on your blog (I know, it's a bit creepy). You should also create one for your opt-in landing page – the place where you're sending people to download your ebook/interview, etc in return for their email (if it's a separate website). Once you have tracking pixels in your sites you can create "custom conversions" on Facebook. This will allow Facebook to track who goes to any of the web pages where you put the piece of code and to deliver ads to them based on their behavior.

On your Facebook Ads account page you go to the top left pulldown menu and go to "all tools" to find Pixels – which is where you will generate tracking pixels and the code that goes in your global header. It's easy (you don't need to know programming or anything) and they will walk you through it. Once your pixels are in place in your global header you're going to create some custom conversions, which you can find under the same pulldown menu.

Say you want to track the people who have read your blog post so that you can serve them ads for your opt-in offer (the free guidebook or whatever). You create a custom audience (in the Audiences section) called "Blog Post Interest" and there create a rule using "URL equals", then put in the full URL for your blog post and select anyone who has gone there in the last 180 days. Then you go to Custom Conversions and you create a custom conversion called something like "Opt-In Conversions". Presumably when people give you their email address and download your content, they will then be sent to a "Thank You Page" (they have been "converted" into a lead). You get the URL for that "Thank You" page and put in the "URL equals" (you have to choose this or it will default to "URL contains", which you don't want). Now you will create an opt-in Facebook ad and the target will INCLUDE your custom audience named "Blog Post Interest" (ie. everyone who has read your blog post) and you will EXCLUDE everyone who has been to your opt-in "Thank You" page – because that means that they've already downloaded your opt-in bribe. No point in paying to keep advertising to them.

You can do the same thing once you market your film to the people who have opted in to your mailing list. On the one hand they are getting your emails promoting the film – on the other they are getting Facebook ads promoting the same offer. You will thus have to create an audience that INCLUDES people who have been to your opt-in "Thank You" page (Opt-In Conversions) but EXCLUDE people who have been to your Film Rental/Purchase Thank You page (Customer conversions) – again you will create a custom conversion for this. It may require two custom conversions if there are different "Thank You" pages for each of a movie rental and a movie sale. In this way you have really fine granular control over to whom your ads are being served, which makes them both more effective and saves you money. It also means that the whole process becomes automated once it's in place.

Once you've created ads and they are being served to the audiences that you've targeted what can you expect? If you've done a good job of targeting your demographic – and there is a responsive demographic for your film – and offered them stuff that they're interested in, you should start to see some results. At first the CPC (cost-per-click) will probably be pretty high (say around $1-$2) as Facebook gets a handle on who is most responsive to your ads. But over a week or two they should start to come down in price. If they don't then re-think your targeting and/or your ad copy.

In general, if you're testing, only change one thing at a time, so that you can know what is and isn't affecting performance. Probably start with the minimal daily budget ($5) and if an ad starts to perform well scale it up slowly. Don't suddenly double the budget; apparently that screws with the Facebook algorithm and could cause you to spend more money for less clicks. I've read that you should never increase your budget by more than 30% in any given 24 hour period. Also, never change your text AND your demographic target AND your budget in one day. Again, those finicky algorithms. Only one thing at a time, please.

This gives you a beginner understanding about how to use Facebook advertising. It really can be quite useful and quite powerful. And relatively simple once you get the hang of it. Expect to lose money at first and so you should decide how much you're willing to lose before you pull the plug (Remember Kenny Rogers). But, if you hit a good interest niche, you could be able to break even and start making a little profit, which you can use to scale up your advertising further to increase your audience and profits and so on. There's no guarantees here. Some audiences are harder to tap than others. Some films don't have a clear niche. But it can give you hope and a strategy to broaden your audience beyond people who know you. If you even manage to get 100 emails and 20 purchases – or five times that – those are people who you can keep in the loop (keeping your leads warm, as they say) so that when you're making your next film, you're starting that much further ahead.

10 THE DIY FILM CAREER

If you've made it this far then I haven't scared you off with all the challenges. Good. I didn't promise that it would be easy or would lead to an Academy Award and a million dollars. But that's not why you should bring your story to life as a film.

You should do it because you *need* to do it and because the other avenues have been cut off to you. It doesn't mean that every film has to be some deeply profound comment on what it means to be human or some burning social issue. We made a silly little movie about a guy who wanted to clone his dead wife. Pursuing your passion can be fun and funny too. What's important is that making movies is your passion, not making enough money to snort coke off the butts of Hollywood escorts (not to be judgy if that's your thing).

It's also important that you don't see this as a one-off thing. In Canada we have a government film-funding agency called Telefilm that has a microbudget film program for films under a certain amount. That's great (though you have to be curated by other schools and organizations to compete for the money, again making it about connections) but the program is only for filmmakers' first films. It's expected that after your one kick at the can you will launch your career and start making million dollar movies afterwards. If only.

You need to see this is as building a DIY Film Career, outside of the usual channels. It would probably be more fruitful to think of your film career like a band thinks of theirs: you need to build an audience over time by creating engaging work and doing the self-marketing necessary. If one of your films gets you a meeting in LA, great. But don't count on it. In fact, assume that it won't happen and instead enjoy the pleasure of making exactly the kinds of movies you want to make in the way that you want to make them.

Even if the first three movies you make suck and are seen by less than 500 people, you will have learned well and truly how to make a feature film. You will have begun to build a body of work. You will be able to call yourself a feature filmmaker. And it will cost you a lot less than film school. Tuition at the American Film Institute is $37,000/year, USC charges $42,000. With crowdfunding to cover your post-production you could make three or four feature films for the cost of one year at film school.

And I want to help you in this. I've seen my fair share of films that have gotten made for commercial reasons and that are, shall we say, not of the highest caliber. I love film and I love the stories that can told through film. I particularly love films that push the boundaries and challenge our taboos and our assumptions. I'm hoping that armed with this book and with some materials to help filmmakers organize their production that the number of these kinds of films will increase. I know that with a little support and mentoring and your own bravery and determination, you will enrich our cinematic culture and it excites me to do my little part in making that happen.

FADE OUT.

ABOUT THE AUTHOR

This is the part where I write about me in the third person as though an important publicist did it for me. Shawn has worked professionally as a development executive for a film production and finance company for over a decade. He has written, directed and co-produced two microbudget feature films and has a terrible made-for-tv movie to his name (which afforded him a very big screen TV). He has also taught screenwriting all over the world and led seminars on nano-budget filmmaking. When he's not doing any of that, he's ghostwriting sci-fi porn involving inter-species sex. Seriously.

Made in the USA
Columbia, SC
15 March 2025